FREE VIDEO

FREE VIDEO

PELLETB Essential Test Tips Video from Trivium Test Prep!

Dear Customer,

Thank you for purchasing from Trivium Test Prep! We're honored to help you prepare for your PELLETB exam.

To show our appreciation, we're offering a **FREE *PELLETB Essential Test Tips* Video by Trivium Test Prep**.* Our video includes 35 test preparation strategies that will make you successful on the PELLETB. All we ask is that you email us your feedback and describe your experience with our product. Amazing, awful, or just so-so: we want to hear what you have to say!

To receive your **FREE *PELLETB Essential Test Tips* Video**, please email us at 5star@ triviumtestprep.com. Include "Free 5 Star" in the subject line and the following information in your email:

1. The title of the product you purchased.
2. Your rating from 1 – 5 (with 5 being the best).
3. Your feedback about the product, including how our materials helped you meet your goals and ways in which we can improve our products.
4. Your full name and shipping address so we can send your **FREE *PELLETB Essential Test Tips* Video**.

If you have any questions or concerns please feel free to contact us directly at 5star@trivium-testprep.com.

Thank you!

– Trivium Test Prep Team

*To get access to the free video please email us at 5star@triviumtestprep.com, and please follow the instructions above.

California Police Officer Exam Study Guide 2019–2020

PELLET B EXAM PREP AND PRACTICE TEST QUESTIONS FOR THE POST ENTRY-LEVEL LAW ENFORCEMENT TEST BATTERY

TABLE OF CONTENTS

INTRODUCTION

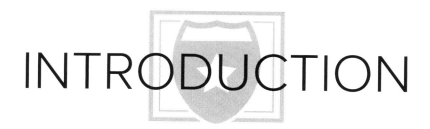

Congratulations on your decision to join the field of law enforcement—few other professions are so rewarding! By purchasing this book, you've already taken the first step toward succeeding in your career. The next step is to do well on the POST Entry-Level Law Enforcement Test Battery (PELLETB), which will require you to demonstrate knowledge of high school–level reading, writing, and reasoning ability.

The Commission on Peace Officer Standards and Training (POST) uses the PELLETB to measure test takers' writing and reading abilities and to determine the likelihood of an examinee's success in law enforcement. It is the gateway for admittance into the basic academy, where you will learn about police procedure and the law. The PELLETB is simply a measure of your communication skills and does not cover police procedure; that is covered in the academy.

This study guide contains a concise but comprehensive review of all sections tested on the PELLETB. It also includes two practice exams, each composed of 65 multiple-choice questions and 40 cloze questions, just like the actual exam. Inside, you will also find tips, tricks, and comprehensive explanations for each testing area. The appendix contains study words related to law enforcement to improve spelling and vocabulary.

TEST FORMAT AND STRATEGIES

The PELLETB consists of 105 questions. All the questions are multiple-choice except for those on the cloze subtest, which uses a fill-in-the-blank format. You will have two hours and thirty minutes to complete the exam.

PELLETB Content

SECTION	SUBTESTS	TOTAL
Writing	Clarity (15) Spelling (15) Vocabulary (15)	45 multiple-choice questions
Reading	Reading comprehension (20) Cloze (40)	60 questions (20 multiple-choice, 40 fill-in-the-blank)
Total	105 questions	2 hours 30 minutes

The test measures reading and writing aptitude over three sections. The first section focuses on writing language ability and tests writing clarity, vocabulary, and spelling. The second section tests reading language ability through reading comprehension.

Writing

The writing section of the exam is divided into three subtests. Each subtest contains fifteen questions as outlined below.

The CLARITY SUBTEST tests grammar and your ability to write concisely and with clarity. The questions are presented as two sentences. You will be prompted to identify and select the sentence that is most clearly and correctly written. This subtest includes only the most common grammatical errors, which will be discussed later in this review.

The SPELLING SUBTEST tests your ability to spell commonly misspelled words. The questions are presented in the form of a sentence with a word missing, designated by a blank space. Keeping the sentence context in mind, you must choose the correctly spelled word option from the list of answer choices. This subtest does not use words from a specific list, so you should study as many common words related to law enforcement as possible. A list of words to study for spelling is included in this book in the appendix.

The VOCABULARY SUBTEST tests your ability to understand words commonly used in law enforcement–related documents and communications. The questions are presented as sentences with one word underlined. You will be prompted to choose the most accurate synonym or definition, given the sentence context, from the answer choices.

This subtest does not use words from a specific list, so you should study as many common words related to law enforcement as possible. As with spelling, lists of common prefixes, suffixes, root words, and vocabulary are provided in this book.

Reading

The reading section of the exam is divided into two subtests: a multiple-choice reading comprehension subtest and the cloze test. This section contains a total of sixty questions: twenty multiple-choice reading comprehension questions and a forty-question cloze test.

The READING COMPREHENSION subtest tests your ability to read and understand what is being communicated in short- and moderate-length passages. The questions are presented after the passage in the form of a "question stem" followed by several answer choices. There will likely be multiple question stems related to one passage. You will be prompted to select answer choices based on the information contained in the passage.

This subtest covers only common concepts. All the information needed to answer questions is contained within the passage.

The CLOZE subtest tests English language proficiency in conjunction with the context of an entire passage. The questions are presented as blank spaces throughout a moderate-length passage. Only the first and last sentences of the passage are complete.

Between those sentences, every seventh word is removed from the passage and replaced with a set of dashed lines. Each dash represents one letter contained in the deleted word. You will be prompted to determine the missing word and fill in the blanks from your own vocabulary, based on the context of the passage. All removed words can be deduced from the context. There *may* be more than one correct choice to fill in a specific blank, but each word choice must be logical and fit within the context of the passage.

TIPS FOR TACKLING MULTIPLE-CHOICE QUESTIONS

The following tips assume you have a basic understanding of test taking: how to follow test proctor instructions, properly record answers, make sure the answer for the right question is recorded, and review an answer sheet before submitting it. If you do nothing else to prepare, learn these quick tips. They will help you focus your efforts and use your time wisely.

Handling Distractors

DISTRACTORS are the incorrect answer choices in a multiple-choice question. They "distract" you from the correct answer. Read and answer the question below:

Criminals are people who violate _____.

(A) Penal Code 62

(B) civil procedure

(C) martial law

(D) criminal laws

The correct answer choice is D, criminal laws. The other, incorrect answer choices—the distractors—are designed to distract the inattentive test taker by "sounding" right or formal. While choices A and C may be partially correct—breaking a specific penal code (criminal) or martial (civilian-imposed military) law may be a crime—neither is the *best* answer choice.

Be sure to read the question for context and tone, and try to determine what is being asked. The preceding question asked for a general definition and used wording from the question as part of the correct answer. While a criminal might violate a *specific* penal code or martial law, generally, violations can be of *any* criminal law. Because criminals are guilty of crimes and *all* criminal laws involve or pertain to crime, choice D is the *best* answer.

Develop a Time Strategy

The examination is two and one-half hours, or 150 minutes, long. If you divide the time equally over the exam, you should have approximately one minute and thirty seconds to answer each question. Pay attention to the time. Note the start and end time for each section prior to beginning. Make a goal to complete each question in one minute or less. One minute seems like a short amount of time, but it actually is not. You will likely complete most questions in less than thirty seconds. Develop your strategy such that you finish the easier questions quickly to allow more time to spend on the difficult questions.

Don't spend too much time on difficult questions. Mark them, skip them, and come back when you have time.

Focus on the Question

Read the question carefully. Words sometimes change meaning based on context. Context is the part of a communication that comes before or after a specific word or passage and provides clarity or meaning. Make sure you read and understand the question before selecting an answer. Read the following sentences:

> The police **<u>arrested</u>** Chad when he was eighteen years old.
>
> Chad is thirty-two years old, but his emotional development was **<u>arrested</u>** when he was eighteen years old.

The word *arrested* is used correctly in both sentences, but it has different meanings depending on the context.

Try to think of an answer before looking at the choices. This can keep you from being distracted by the incorrect answer choices and help you more easily identify the answer.

Correct is Not Always Best

Several answers could be *correct*, or close to correct, but you must choose the *best* answer choice. Beware of answer choices that are close to the correct answer but are merely distractions.

Use the Process of Elimination

Eliminate answer choices you know are incorrect. Choose your answer from the remaining choices.

For "All of the Above" and "None of the Above" answer choices, look for choices that include elements that break the "All" or "None" rule, such as a true element in a group of false elements or vice versa. If one element does not belong with the rest of the group's elements, then the answer cannot be *all*, or *none*, of the above.

Reread the question and remaining answers and select an answer choice.

SCORING

Your raw score (the number of questions you answer correctly) will be converted into your **T-score**. Simply put, the T-score reflects how well you did against everyone else who took the test. POST provides a distribution, or a bell-shaped curve, with a midpoint, or average, of 50 and a standard deviation of 10. A T-score of 50 reflects average performance compared to all the other applicants who took the test. A score of 40 or below would be below average. A T-score of 60 or above is above average. There is no "passing" score; agencies and academies require different scores, so check with yours to determine your target T-score.

You will receive a score report that details the number of questions you answered correctly in each section and that also gives your percentile rank, which shows how you did in comparison with other test takers. Each agency has its own entrance requirements, so be sure to check the requirements of the institutions you want to attend so you can set appropriate goals for yourself.

ADMINISTRATION AND TEST DAY

The PELLETB is administered by POST-participating law enforcement agencies and academies, not by POST itself. To register for the exam, you must directly contact the participating agency or academy where you are applying. The PELLETB is a pencil-and-paper test; it is not offered as a computer-administered test, nor is it available online. You must test at a location in the state of California.

There is no penalty for guessing, so if you do not know the answer to a question, guess. You may get it right! Guesswork is still a matter of deduction; eliminate as many choices as possible before making a guess between the remaining answers.

On test day, arrive early. Check with the facility or participating agency to make sure you know what type of identification to bring (usually government-issued photo identification). Bring at least two sharpened No. 2 pencils. Personal belongings, cell phones, and other electronic, photographic, recording, or listening devices are not permitted in the testing center. Many testing centers offer lockers to secure your personal items, but you should check beforehand with the facility to be sure storage is available.

You may test only once in a thirty-day period; you may retest on the thirty-first day or later. If you retest within thirty days with a different agency, your test results will be invalidated.

For more information, visit https://post.ca.gov/LE-Entry-Level-Test-Battery-Applicant-FAQs.

About Trivium Test Prep

Trivium Test Prep uses industry professionals with decades' worth of knowledge in their fields, proven with degrees and honors in law, medicine, business, education, the military, and more, to produce high-quality test prep books for students.

Our study guides are specifically designed to increase any student's score. Our books are also shorter and more concise than typical study guides, so you can increase your score while significantly decreasing your study time.

How to Use This Guide

This guide is not meant to waste your time on superfluous information or concepts you've already learned. Instead, we hope you use this guide to focus on the concepts *you* need to master for the test and to develop critical test-taking skills. To support this effort, the guide provides:

- organized concepts with detailed explanations
- practice questions with worked-through solutions
- key test-taking strategies
- simulated one-on-one tutor experience
- tips, tricks, and test secrets

Because we have eliminated filler and fluff, you'll be able to work through the guide at a significantly faster pace than you would with other test prep books. By allowing you to focus only on those concepts that will increase your score, we'll make your study time shorter and more effective.

The chapters in this book are divided into a review of the topics covered on the exam. This is not intended to teach you everything you'll see on the test: there is no way to cram all that material into one book! Instead, we are going to help you recall information that you've already learned, and, even more importantly, we'll show you how to apply that knowledge. Each chapter includes an extensive review with practice questions to test your knowledge. With time, practice, and determination, you'll be well prepared for test day.

PART I: REVIEW

WRITING

INTRODUCTION

Written and verbal communications are equally important in law enforcement. Writing accurate, clear, and concise memos, warrants, and police reports ensures that the information provided is as the officer intended. Unclear or confusing verbal communication can create misunderstanding and even danger if an officer is attempting to control a volatile situation. The same is true of written work. Wordy, incoherent, error-laden communications create confusion.

The PELLETB specifically tests three aspects of writing: clarity, vocabulary, and spelling.

Clear and concise writing helps readers easily understand a message. In law enforcement, the last thing an officer wishes is for lawyers, juries, or the public to have to *guess* what he or she meant in a report or other written communication. Cases have been won and lost based on officer testimony related to a well-written or poorly written report.

Inspect the following two passages as an example of how wordiness and grammatical errors can confuse communication.

PASSAGE ONE

On Friday, August 17, 2014, about 1530 hours while working as a patrol officer in full uniform in Sector 2 of River City I heard over my car radio that Officer Smith had two people in front of Superior Court with warrants. I arrived at the Superior Court and met with Officer Smith. Officer Smith told me a woman, identified as Jane Johnson, and a man, identified as Ronald Jones, were at the courthouse. Jane and Ronald were at the court for a family hearing.

A records check with River City Records and Warrants confirmed Jane had a misdemeanor warrant, and Ronald had a felony warrant, out of River City.

Jane and Ronald were arrested without incident to answer for the warrant.

On Friday, August 17, 2014, about 1530 hours I contacted Jane Johnson and Ronald Jones in front of the River City Superior Court. Jane and Ronald were at the court for a family hearing. I had information both parties had active warrants for their arrest.

A records check with River City Records and Warrants confirmed Jane had an active misdemeanor warrant for her arrest and Ronald had an active felony warrant for his arrest, both issued by River City.

I arrested Jane and Ronald without incident to answer for their warrants.

Isn't it much easier to understand passage two? Are the sentences clear, concise, and grammatically correct, and do they contain all the necessary information? On the other hand, does passage one seem wordy and filled with grammatical errors? Is it clear or confusing? Unclear reports of search warrants could lead to poor investigations, arrests, and prosecutions.

The Clarity subsection of the PELLETB tests only common grammatical mistakes and requires the test taker to identify the most clearly written of two sentences. Knowing the rules of grammar, mechanics, and sentence structure will help you identify the correct answer on the PELLETB. Furthermore, avoiding common errors can help add clarity to your written communication. We review the basics and common mistakes in this chapter.

The other two subsections—Vocabulary and Spelling—ask you to define and spell words. Two sections of this chapter focus on building your vocabulary, determining the meaning of unfamiliar words, and reviewing spelling rules.

THE PARTS OF SPEECH

NOUNS are the words that describe people, places, things, and ideas. The subject of a sentence is typically a noun. For example, in the sentence "The station was very clean," the subject, *station*, is a noun; it is a place.

Nouns have several subcategories: common nouns (*chair, car, house*), proper nouns (*Julie, David*), noncountable nouns (*money, water*), and countable nouns (*dollars, cubes*), among others. There is much crossover among these subcategories (for example, *chair* is both common and countable), and other subcategories do exist.

SINGULAR PRONOUNS
- I, me, my, mine
- you, your, yours
- he, him, his
- she, her, hers
- it, its

PLURAL PRONOUNS
- we, us, our, ours
- they, them, their, theirs

PRONOUNS replace nouns in a sentence or paragraph, allowing a writer to achieve a smooth flow throughout a text by avoiding unnecessary repetition. While there are countless nouns in the English language, there are only a few types of pronouns. Take the sentence "Sam stayed home from school because Sam was not feeling well." The noun *Sam* appears twice in the same sentence. Instead, the pronoun *he* can be used to stand in for *Sam*: "Sam stayed home from school because he was not feeling well."

VERBS express action (*run, jump, play*) or state of being (*is, seems*). Verbs that describe action are **ACTION VERBS**, and those that describe being are **LINKING VERBS**.

ACTION: My brother <u>plays</u> tennis.

LINKING: He is the best player on the team.

ADJECTIVES provide more information about a noun in a sentence. Take the sentence "The boy hit the ball." If you want your readers to know more about the noun *boy*, you could use an adjective to describe him: *the little boy, the young boy, the tall boy*.

ADVERBS describe verbs, adjectives, and even other adverbs. For example, in the sentence "The doctor had recently hired a new employee," the adverb *recently* tells us more about how the action *hired* took place.

> ⚠
> Participles are nouns or adjectives formed by adding –ed or –ing to a verb.
> <u>Seated</u> politely, Ron listened to his friend's boring story.
> Maya petted the <u>sleeping</u> cat.

PREPOSITIONS express the location of a noun or pronoun in relation to other words and phrases described in a sentence. For example, in the sentence "The nurse parked her car in a parking garage," the preposition *in* describes the position of the car in relation to the garage. Together, the preposition and the noun that follow it are called a **PREPOSITIONAL PHRASE**. In this example, the prepositional phrase is *in a parking garage*.

CONJUNCTIONS connect words, phrases, and clauses. **INTERJECTIONS**, like *wow* and *hey*, express emotion and are most commonly used in conversation and casual writing.

Examples

1. Which of the following lists includes all the nouns in the following sentence?

   I have lived in Minnesota since August, but I still don't own a warm coat or gloves.

   (A) coat, gloves

   (B) I, coat, gloves

   (C) Minnesota, August, coat, gloves

   (D) I, Minnesota, August, warm, coat, gloves

2. Which of the following lists includes all the adjectives in the following sentence?

   The new chef carefully stirred the boiling soup and then lowered the heat.

   (A) new, boiling

   (B) new, carefully, boiling

   (C) new, carefully, boiling, heat

   (D) new, carefully, boiling, lowered, heat

3. Choose the word that best completes the sentence.

   Her love _____ blueberry muffins kept her coming back to the bakery every week.

   (A) to

   (B) with

   (C) of

   (D) about

PUNCTUATION

The basic rules for using the major punctuation marks are given in the table below.

Table 1.1. Using Punctuation

PUNCTUATION	PURPOSE	EXAMPLE
Period	Ending sentences	Periods go at the end of complete sentences.
Question mark	Ending questions	What's the best way to end a sentence?
Exclamation point	Ending sentences that show extreme emotion	I'll never understand how to use commas!
Comma	Joining two independent clauses (always with a coordinating conjunction)	Commas can be used to join clauses, but they must always be followed by a coordinating conjunction.
	Setting apart introductory and nonessential words and phrases	Commas, when used properly, set apart extra information in a sentence.
	Separating items in a list	My favorite punctuation marks include the colon, semicolon, and period.
Semicolon	Joining together two independent clauses (never used with a conjunction)	I love exclamation points; they make sentences seem so exciting!
Colon	Introducing a list, explanation, or definition	When I see a colon, I know what to expect: more information.
Apostrophe	Forming contractions	It's amazing how many people can't use apostrophes correctly.
	Showing possession	Parentheses are my sister's favorite punctuation; she finds commas' rules confusing.
Quotation marks	Indicating a direct quote	I said to her, "Tell me more about parentheses."

Examples

4. Which of the following sentences contains an error in punctuation?
    (A) I love apple pie! John exclaimed with a smile.
    (B) Jennifer loves Adam's new haircut.
    (C) Billy went to the store; he bought bread, milk, and cheese.
    (D) Alexandra hates raisins, but she loves chocolate chips.

5. Sam, do you want to come with us for dinner_
    Which punctuation mark correctly completes the sentence?
    (A) .
    (B) ?
    (C) ;
    (D) :

PHRASES

Understanding subjects and predicates is key to understanding what a phrase is. The SUBJECT is what the sentence is about; the PREDICATE contains the verb and its modifiers.

> The nurse at the front desk will answer any questions you have.
>
> SUBJECT: the nurse at the front desk
>
> PREDICATE: will answer any questions you have

A PHRASE is a group of words that communicates only part of an idea because it lacks either a subject or a predicate. Phrases can begin with prepositions, verbs, nouns, or participles.

> PREPOSITIONAL PHRASE: The dog is hiding under the porch.
>
> VERB PHRASE: The chef wanted to cook a different dish.
>
> NOUN PHRASE: The big red barn rests beside the vacant chicken house.
>
> PARTICIPIAL PHRASE: Walking quietly, she tried not to wake the baby.

Example

Identify the type of phrase underlined in the following sentence:

6. The experienced paraprofessional worked independently with the eager students.
    (A) prepositional phrase
    (B) noun phrase
    (C) verb phrase
    (D) participial phrase

CLAUSES

CLAUSES contain both a subject and a predicate. They can be either independent or dependent. An INDEPENDENT (or main) CLAUSE can stand alone as its own sentence.

> The dog ate her homework.

DEPENDENT (or subordinate) CLAUSES cannot stand alone as their own sentences. They start with a subordinating conjunction, relative pronoun, or relative adjective, which will make them sound incomplete.

> Because the dog ate her homework

Clauses can be joined together to create more complex sentences. COORDINATING CONJUNCTIONS join two independent clauses, and SUBORDINATING CONJUNCTIONS join an independent to a dependent clause.

Table 1.2. Conjunctions

Coordinating	for, and, nor, but, or, yet, so (FANBOYS)	The nurse prepared the patient for surgery, and the doctor performed the surgery.
Subordinating	after, although, because, if, since, so that, though, until, when, while	She had to ride the subway because her car was being serviced.

Example

Choose the word that best completes the sentence.

7. Christine left her house early on Monday morning, _____ she was still late for work.
    (A) but
    (B) and
    (C) for
    (D) or

COMMON GRAMMATICAL ERRORS

Pronoun-Antecedent Agreement

Pronouns must agree with their ANTECEDENTS (the words they replace) in number; however, some pronouns also require gender agreement (*him, her*). PRONOUN-ANTECEDENT AGREEMENT rules can be found below:

1. Antecedents joined by *and* typically require a plural pronoun.
    The children and their dogs enjoyed their day at the beach.
    If the two nouns refer to the same person, a singular pronoun is preferable.
    My best friend and confidant still lives in her log cabin.

2. For compound antecedents joined by *or*, the pronoun agrees with the nearer or nearest antecedent.
    Either the resident mice or the manager's cat gets itself a meal of good leftovers.

3. When indefinite pronouns function in a sentence, the pronoun must agree with the number of the indefinite pronoun.
    Neither student finished his or her assignment.
    Both students finished their assignments.

4. When collective nouns function as antecedents, the pronoun choice will be singular or plural depending on the function of the collective.
    The audience was cheering as it rose to its feet in unison.
    Our family are spending their vacations in Maine, Hawaii, and Rome.

5. When each and every precede the antecedent, the pronoun agreement will be singular.
    Each and every man, woman, and child brings unique qualities to his or her family.

Every creative writer, technical writer, and research writer is attending his or her assigned lecture.

How would you complete the following sentence? "Every boy and girl should check _____ homework before turning it in." Many people would use the pronoun *their*. But since the antecedent is "every boy and girl," technically, the correct answer would be *his or her*. Using *they* or *their* in similar situations is increasingly accepted in formal speech, however. It is unlikely that you will see questions like this on the PELLETB, but if you do, it is safest to use the technically correct response.

Example

8. In which of the following sentences do the nouns and pronouns NOT agree?

    (A) After we walked inside, we took off our hats and shoes and hung them in the closet.

    (B) The members of the band should leave her instruments in the rehearsal room.

    (C) The janitor on duty should rinse out his or her mop before leaving for the day.

    (D) When you see someone in trouble, you should always try to help them.

Vague or Unclear Pronouns

A vague or unclear reference is generally the result of a PRONOUN ERROR. Pronoun errors occur when it is not clear what the antecedent of a pronoun is—the word it replaces. In the first sentence below, it is difficult to determine whose notes the officer gave to the Assistant District Attorney. Do the notes belong to the officer or to the ADA? The antecedent of the pronoun *his* is unclear. To improve this sentence, be sure the pronoun refers to only one antecedent noun.

> WRONG: Officer Lane gave Assistant District Attorney Poole his notes.
>
> CORRECT: Officer Lane gave his notes to Assistant District Attorney Poole.

Another way to ensure clarity in writing is to avoid using pronouns to refer to an implied idea; it is better to state the idea explicitly. In the sentence below, the writer misuses the pronoun *it*. The reader might be confused: did jury deliberation take a long time, or did the process of the trial take a long time? To improve this sentence, the writer should state the idea explicitly, avoiding a pronoun altogether.

> WRONG: The jury reached a verdict in the defendant's case, but it took a long time.
>
> CORRECT: The jury reached a verdict in the defendant's case, but the deliberations took a long time.

Example

9. Choose the more clearly written sentence.

    (A) John said he and Frank were fighting when he was shot.

    (B) John said he and Frank were fighting when Frank was shot.

Subject-Verb Agreement

Verbs are conjugated to indicate PERSON, which refers to the point of view of the sentence. First person is the speaker (*I, we*); second person is the person being addressed (*you*); and third person is outside the conversation (*they, them*). Verbs are also conjugated to match the NUMBER (singular or plural) of their subject. HELPING VERBS (*to be, to have, to do*) are used to conjugate verbs. An unconjugated verb is called an INFINITIVE and includes the word *to* in front of it (*to be, to break*).

Table 1.3. Verb Conjugation (Present Tense)

PERSON	SINGULAR	PLURAL
First person	I give	we give
Second person	you give	you (all) give
Third person	he/she/it gives	they give

Verbs must agree in number with their subjects. (In some other languages, such as Spanish, verbs must also agree with their subjects in gender.) SUBJECT-VERB AGREEMENT rules follow:

1. Singular subjects agree with singular verbs; plural subjects agree with plural verbs.
    The girl walks her dog.
    The girls walk their dogs.

2. Compound subjects joined by *and* typically take a plural verb unless they are considered one item.
    Correctness and precision are required for all good writing.
    Macaroni and cheese makes a great snack for children.

3. Compound subjects joined by *or* or *nor* agree with the nearer or nearest subject.
    Neither I nor my friends are looking forward to our final exams.
    Neither my friends nor I am looking forward to our final exams.

4. All singular indefinite pronouns agree with singular verbs.
    Neither of the students is happy about the play.
    Each of the many cars is on the grass.
    Every one of the administrators speaks highly of Officer Larkin.

5. All plural indefinite pronouns agree with plural verbs.
    Several of the students are happy about the play.
    Both of the cars are on the grass.
    Many of the administrators speak highly of Officer Larkin.

6. Some of the singular indefinite pronouns (*all, most, some, more, any*) change agreement depending on the object of the preposition.
    All of the pie is gone.
    All of the pies are gone.
    Some of the bucket is dirty.
    Some of the buckets are dirty.

7. Collective nouns agree with singular verbs when the collective acts as one unit. Collective nouns agree with plural verbs when the collective acts as individuals within the group.

The <u>jury announces</u> its decision after sequestration. (*They act as one unit.*)

The <u>jury make</u> phone calls during their break time. (*They act as individuals.*)

8. Nouns that are plural in form but singular in meaning will agree with singular verbs.
<u>Measles is</u> a painful disease.
<u>Sixty dollars is</u> too much to pay for that book.

9. Singular verbs come after titles, business corporations, and words used as terms.
<u>"Three Little Kittens" is</u> a favorite nursery rhyme for many children.
<u>General Motors is</u> a major employer for the city.

> ⚠ Ignore words between the subject and the verb when trying to match a subject and verb:
>
> The new <u>library</u> ~~with its many books and rooms~~ <u>fills</u> a long-felt need.

Example

10. Which of the following sentences contains a subject-verb error?
   (A) The witness and her mother are asked to remain seated.
   (B) Some of the officers at the station is planning to stay late.
   (C) My partner and I are happy with the new schedule.
   (D) The department is hiring for many new positions this year.

Verb Tense Agreement

Verbs are also conjugated to indicate TENSE, or when the action has happened. Actions can happen in the past, present, or future. Tense also describes over how long a period the action took place.

- SIMPLE verbs describe general truths or something that happened once.
- CONTINUOUS verbs describe an ongoing action.
- PERFECT verbs describe repeated actions or actions that started in the past and have been completed.
- PERFECT CONTINUOUS verbs describe actions that started in the past and are continuing.

Table 1.4. Verb Tenses

TENSE	PAST	PRESENT	FUTURE
Simple	I <u>gave</u> her a gift yesterday.	I <u>give</u> her a gift every day.	I <u>will give</u> her a gift on her birthday.
Continuous	I <u>was giving</u> her a gift when you got here.	I <u>am giving</u> her a gift; come in!	I <u>will be giving</u> her a gift at dinner.
Perfect	I <u>had given</u> her a gift before you got there.	I <u>have given</u> her a gift already.	I <u>will have given</u> her a gift by midnight.
Perfect continuous	Her friends <u>had been giving</u> her gifts all night when I arrived.	I <u>have been giving</u> her gifts every year for nine years.	I <u>will have been giving</u> her gifts on holidays for ten years next year.

The verb tenses in a sentence must agree with each other and with the other information provided in the sentence. Pay attention to words like *before, after, tomorrow, yesterday, then,* and *next,* which describe when in time events occurred.

> **WRONG**: After he changed clothes, the officer will be ready to go home.
>
> **CORRECT**: After he changed clothes, the officer was ready to go home.

In the example above, the introductory phrase describes an action that was completed in the past (*he changed*), so the rest of the sentence should also be in the past (*was ready*).

Example

11. Which verb phrase best completes the sentence?

By this time tomorrow, we _____ in New York.

(A) will have arrived

(B) have arrived

(C) arrive

(D) was arriving

Comparing Adjectives and Adverbs

The suffix *–er* is used when comparing two things, and the suffix *–est* is used when comparing more than two. Adjectives longer than two syllables are compared using *more* (for two things) or *most* (for three or more things).

> Anne is taller than Steve, but Steve is more coordinated.
>
> Of the five brothers, Billy is the funniest, and Alex is the most intelligent.

More and *most* should NOT be used in conjunction with *–er* and *–est* endings.

> **WRONG**: My most warmest sweater is made of wool.
>
> **CORRECT**: My warmest sweater is made of wool.

Example

12. Which of the following sentences contains an adjective error?

(A) The new red car was faster than the old blue car.

(B) Reggie's apartment is in the tallest building on the block.

(C) The slice of cake was tastier than the brownie.

(D) Of the four speeches, Jerry's was the most long.

Misplaced Modifiers

A **MODIFIER** is a word or phrase—like an adjective—that adds detail to a sentence. Adjectives, adverbs, and modifying phrases should be placed as close as possible to the word they modify. **MISPLACED MODIFIERS** can create confusing or nonsensical sentences.

> **WRONG**: Running down the alley, the siren sounded and the police officer knew backup had arrived.
>
> **CORRECT**: Running down the alley, the police officer heard the siren and knew backup had arrived.

In the first example above, the phrase "running down the alley" looks like it is modifying "the siren." For clarity, it should be placed next to "the police officer," the noun it modifies.

> **WRONG:** Describing the crime, the jury listened to the prosecutor deliver his opening statement.
>
> **CORRECT:** The jury listened to the prosecutor deliver his opening statement describing the crime.

In this example, the phrase "describing the crime" is first placed next to the word "jury," making it seem like the jury is describing the crime. To fix the sentence, the modifier should be moved so it is clear that the prosecutor is describing the crime.

Example

13. Choose the more clearly written sentence.

(A) During police contacts, failure to follow directions is often the cause of officer uses of force.

(B) During police contacts, failure to follow directions often is the cause of officer uses of force.

Sentence Fragments

A sentence fragment occurs when a group of words is followed by a period but does not form a complete sentence or thought. A sentence fragment can be corrected by turning it into a complete sentence that has at least one independent clause.

> **WRONG:** Because he was tired of presiding over cases involving the same criminals in his courtroom.
>
> **CORRECT:** The judge left the bench because he was tired of presiding over cases involving the same criminals in his courtroom.

Example

14. Choose the more clearly written sentence.

(A) The suspect robbed an elderly woman and then fled the scene in a red sedan heading northbound on Eighth Avenue.

(B) The suspect robbed an elderly woman and then fled the scene in a red sedan. Heading northbound on Eighth Avenue.

Run-on Sentences

A RUN-ON SENTENCE is two or more complete sentences not separated by appropriate punctuation, such as a comma, period, or semicolon. For example, the following is a run-on sentence: "Jack shot his friend Mark over a pool game, Jack was mad because he thought Mark was cheating."

Be sure to separate each complete thought with proper punctuation. Applying this rule changes the preceding sentence: "Jack shot his friend Mark over a pool game. Jack was mad because he thought Mark was cheating."

15. Choose the more clearly written sentence.

(A) Jane broke into the house intending to steal items to exchange for drugs she activated the alarm and ran away.

(B) Jane broke into the house intending to steal items to exchange for drugs. She activated the alarm and ran away.

VOCABULARY

Vocabulary is a collection of words used or known in language. Possessing a large vocabulary can help you better understand communications. It can improve your ability to determine context and add clarity to the written or spoken word. Law enforcement vocabulary can be very technical, but it also contains many commonly used words. The vocabulary section of the PELLETB measures ability to understand and appropriately use *common* words.

On the PELLETB, each question is structured as one sentence with a word underlined. The answer choices list alternative words to replace the underlined word. You must choose the word that most closely matches the meaning of the underlined word.

Developing a large vocabulary takes time and practice; it cannot be done overnight. However, studying commonly used words and their synonyms can help. Synonyms are words that share the same or nearly the same meaning as other words. Understanding word roots, prefixes, suffixes, and how they affect words can also help you determine the meaning of unfamiliar words based on the word's structure.

Root Words

A ROOT WORD is the base of a word. It comes after a prefix or before a suffix. In English, many root words come from ancient Greek and Latin. Root words hold meaning and can stand alone as words. Learning to recognize common root words can help you build your vocabulary and make educated guesses about unfamiliar words. It can also help improve your ability to comprehend various types of communications.

Table 1.5 lists some common root words, their meanings, and examples.

Table 1.5. Common Root Words

ROOT	MEANING	EXAMPLES
actus, act	drive, lead, act	active, action, activate, react
acurer	to sharpen	acute, acumen, acuity
agon	contest, struggle	antagonist, agony
ambi	both	ambiguous, ambidextrous
anthropo	man, human, humanity	anthropologist, philanthropist
aqua	water	aquarium, aquatic
arbit	judge	arbitrary, arbitration
archos, arch	chief, first, rule	monarch, archangel, anarchy
aud	to hear	audience, audible, auditory
auto	self	autobiography, autograph, autoimmune, automobile

ROOT	MEANING	EXAMPLES
bene	good	benevolent, beneficial
bio	life	biology, biography
capere, cip, cept	take, seize	captive, capture, captivate, intercept
cedere, ced	to go, yield	recede, precede, exceed, predecessor
chron	time	chronological, chronic, synchronize
circum	around	circumference, circumvent, circumscribe
clino, clin	lean, slant	incline, decline, inclination, recline
contra, counter	against	contradict, contrary, counteract
cred	believe	creed, incredible
crit	judge	criticize, critical
crypto, crypt	hide, conceal	cryptic, cryptogram, encryption
dict	to say	dictation, dictate, predict
duc, duct	to lead	conduct, induce, induct
dyna	power	dynamic, dynamite, dynamo
dys	bad, hard, unlucky	dysfunctional, dyslexic, dystopia
equ	equal, even	equidistant, inequity, equivalent, equitable
errare, err, errat	wander, go astray	errant, err, erratic, aberration
fac	to do, to make	factory, manufacture, artifact
finis, fin	end, limit	final, definite, infinite
form	shape	conform, reform
fort	strength	fortitude, fortress, fortify, comfort
fract	to break	fracture, fraction
gno, gnos	know	diagnosis, ignore, incognito, cognitive
gram	something written	telegram, diagram, grammar
graph	writing	graphic, autograph
gravis, grav, griev	heavy, serious	grave, grievance, grievous, aggravate, gravity
hetero	different	heteronym, heterogeneous
homo	same	homonym, homogenous
hydro	water	hydrate, dehydrate, hydraulic
hypo	below, beneath	hypothermia, hypothetical, hypoglycemic
ject	throw	eject, project, reject
jud	judge	judicial, prejudice
jus, jur, just	right, law, oath	abjure, perjury, conjure, jury, jurisprudence
juven	young	juvenile, rejuvenate
mal	bad	malfeasance, malevolent, malcontent
mater	mother	maternal, maternity
meter, metr	measure	thermometer, perimeter, metric
micro	small	microbe, microscope, microchip
mis, miso	hate, wrong	misanthrope, misogyny, misbehave

Table 1.5. Common Root Words (continued)

ROOT	MEANING	EXAMPLES
mono	one	monologue, monotonous, monotheism
morph	form, shape	morphology, metamorphosis
mort	death	mortal, mortician, immortal
multi	many	multimedia, multiple, multiply, multicolored
nym	name	antonym, synonym, homonym
onus, oner	burden	onerous, onus, exonerate
opsis, optic	sight, eye, view	optical, synopsis
pater	father	paternal, paternity
phil	love	philanthropist, philosophy
phobia	fear	claustrophobia, acrophobia, phobic
phon	sound	cacophony, phonetic, symphony
photo, phos	light	photograph, photogenic, phosphorous
placaere	appease	placate, placid
port	to carry	portable, transportation, export
pretiare, prec	to value	precious, deprecation, depreciation, appreciation
pseudo	false	pseudonym, pseudoscience
psycho	soul, spirit	psychology, psychic, psychotic
rupt	to break	bankrupt, disrupt, erupt
scope	to watch, see	microscope, telescope
scrib, scribe	to write	inscribe, prescribe, describe
sect, sec	to cut	bisect, section, intersect, dissect
sentire, sent	to feel, perceive	consent, resent, sentient, sentiment
skep, scop	examine	skeptical, scope
spect	to look	inspect, spectator, circumspect, retrospective
struct	to build	construct, destruct, restructure, infrastructure
tacere, tac, tic	to be silent	tacit, taciturn, reticent
techno	art, science, skill	technique, technology
tele	far off	television, telephone, teleport
tendere	stretch	extend, tend, distend
terrere, terr	frighten	deter, terror, terrorism
therm	heat	thermal, thermometer, thermos
thesis	position	synthesis, hypothesis
venire, veni, ven	come, move toward	convention, contravene, intervene
vid, vis	to see	video, envision, evident, vision
voc	to call	voice, vocalize, advocate
zelos	ardor	zeal, zealous, zealot

Prefixes

PREFIXES are sets of letters that are added to the beginning of a word. Adding a prefix to a word can change its meaning. For instance, if you take the root word *jud*, which means *judge*, and add the prefix *pre–*, which means *before*, you create the word *prejudice*, which means to prejudge.

Prefixes cannot stand on their own as words, but they do hold meaning. Learning to recognize common prefixes builds vocabulary and helps readers make educated guesses about unfamiliar words. It can also help improve reading comprehension in general.

Table 1.6 lists some common prefixes, their meanings, and examples.

Table 1.6. Common Prefixes

PREFIX	MEANING	EXAMPLES
ambi–, amb–	around, on both sides	ambiguous, ambivalent
anti–	against, opposite	anticlimactic, antiseptic
bi–	two	bicycle, bifocals, bilingual
circum–, circa–	around, about	circumference, circadian, circumvent
com–, con–	with	communicate, convince
contra–	against	contradict, contrary, contravene
de–	reduce, remove	devalue, decelerate, decompose
di, dis–	not, opposite of	discontinue, disappear, discover, digress
en–, em–	cause to, into	enact, empower, embrace, enclose
fore–	before, front of	foreshadow, forebear
il–, im–, in–, ir–	not, without	illegal, impossible, invalidate, irresponsible
im–, in–	in, into	import, income
inter–	between, among	interrupt, intercept, intercede
mid–	middle	midterm, midway
mis–	bad, wrong	misinterpret, misspell
non–	not, without	nonconformist, nonfiction, nonviolent
over–	excessive	overeat, overconfident
peri–	around, about	perimeter, periphery
pre–	before	preexisting, precedent, preview
re–, red–	again, back, against, behind	recede, redo, retreat, rewrite
semi–	half, partial	semiconscious, semicircle
sub–	under	subway, submarine
super–	above, beyond	superfluous, superhuman, superior
trans–	across, over, through, beyond	transmit, transgression, transit
un–	not, opposite of	unusual, unashamed, unfair

Suffixes

SUFFIXES are the same as prefixes except that suffixes are added to the ends of words rather than the beginnings.

Table 1.7 lists some common prefixes, their meanings, and examples.

Table 1.7. Common Suffixes

SUFFIX	MEANING	EXAMPLES
–able, –ible	is, can be	excitable, moveable, collectible
–al, –ial	having characteristics of, pertaining to	facial, procedural, universal
–cide, –cidum	kill	homicide, insecticide
–ed	past tense	arrested, called, treated
–en	made of, to cause to be	awaken, frighten, weaken
–er, –or	a person who	pioneer, professor, volunteer
–er	more	taller, meaner, shorter
–est	the most	fastest, meanest, shortest
–ful	full of	helpful, shameful, thankful
–ic	relating to, having characteristics of	poetic, dogmatic, organic
–ing	present participles, materials	sleeping, eating, bedding, frosting
–ion, –tion, –ation, –sion	act, process	submission, celebration, navigation
–ity, –cy –ty	state of, condition	activity, civility, normalcy, society
–ive, –ative, –itive	quality of	active, qualitative, sensitive
–ize	to make (forms verb)	compartmentalize, mechanize
–less	without	blameless, homeless, remorseless
–ly	in the manner of	bravely, courageously, horrifically
–ment	state of being, act of	contentment, placement, resentment
–ness	state of, condition of	weakness, kindness
–ology	study	biology, physiology, sociology
–ous, –eous, –ious	having qualities of, full of	riotous, hazardous, righteous, gracious
–y	characterized by	sassy, cheeky, slimy

Examples

In the following questions, choose the word from the answer choices that is closest in meaning to the underlined word.

16. The suspect did not have any <u>OUTSTANDING</u> warrants.
    (A) inactive
    (B) unsettled
    (C) unconfirmed
    (D) confirmed

17. Because a career in law enforcement can be dangerous, officers should not become <u>COMPLACENT</u>.
- **(A)** confident
- **(B)** unsafe
- **(C)** self-satisfied
- **(D)** cheerful

18. During her testimony, the witness <u>RECANTED</u> her statement.
- **(A)** affirmed
- **(B)** rescinded
- **(C)** retold
- **(D)** regretted

19. The jury did not believe the suspect's mother was a <u>CREDIBLE</u> witness.
- **(A)** trustworthy
- **(B)** likeable
- **(C)** suitable
- **(D)** useful

20. The suspect's account of the incident was full of <u>DISCREPANCIES</u>.
- **(A)** falsities
- **(B)** inaccuracies
- **(C)** deception
- **(D)** inconsistencies

SPELLING

Why is spelling important in law enforcement? Much of what officers write is by hand, at least initially. What's more, any notes or other material an officer writes in connection with a crime or criminal investigation is *discoverable*. That means the court can compel an officer to turn over his or her notes and communications to the court and lawyers for both sides. Right or wrong, spelling could affect the officer's credibility and competence in the eyes of a jury. Many people believe multiple spelling and grammatical errors show a lack of attention to detail and a tendency toward sloppy work. Both are detrimental to effective police work.

Thankfully, spelling is the easiest part of the examination to study for. And while you could relegate yourself to simply repetitively writing random words on a piece of paper like you did after school when you were in trouble with the teacher, there are more focused methods to improve your performance on a multiple-choice spelling test. It can help to learn the following tips, tricks, and rules to prevent common spelling errors.

Homophones

HOMOPHONES are words that sound alike but are spelled differently and hold different meanings, such as *break* and *brake*.

> Officer Brady stepped on the <u>brake</u> to stop the car.
> Officer Brady took a lunch <u>break</u> during his shift.

Commonly confused words include:

- **ACCEPT**: agree
  EXCEPT: not including

- **ALOUD**: said out loud
  ALLOWED: able to

- **BARE**: uncovered
  BEAR: large animal; to carry

- **BRAKE**: to stop
  BREAK: to damage or interrupt

- **DIE**: to no longer be alive
  DYE: to artificially change color

- **EFFECT**: result (noun)
  AFFECT: to change (verb)

- **FLOUR**: used for cooking
  FLOWER: grows out of the ground

- **HEAL**: to get better
  HEEL: the back part of the foot

- **HOLE**: an opening
  WHOLE: all of something

- **INSURE**: to have insurance (*I need to insure my car.*)
  ENSURE: to make sure something happens (*She ensured that the dog found a good home.*)

- **MEAT**: the flesh of an animal
  MEET: to see someone

- **MORNING**: the start of the day
  MOURNING: grieving

- **PATIENCE**: tolerating annoyances
  PATIENTS: people receiving medical care

- **PEACE**: not at war
  PIECE: a part of something

- **POOR**: having very little money
  POUR: to dispense from a container

- **PRINCIPAL**: the leader or administrative head of a school
  PRINCIPLE: a strongly held belief

- **RAIN**: precipitation
  REIN: a strap that controls an animal
  REIGN: to rule over

- **RIGHT**: correct; a legal entitlement
  RITE: a ritual
  WRITE: to put words on paper

- **STAIR**: used to get from one floor to another
  STARE: a long, fixed look

- **SUITE**: a set of rooms
  SWEET: the taste associated with sugar

- **THEIR**: belonging to them (*they brought their luggage*)
  THERE: a place (*the luggage is over there*)
  THEY'RE: they are (*they're looking for the luggage*)

- **THROUGH**: to go in one side and out the other
  THREW: tossed (past tense of *throw*)

- **TO**: the preposition indicating movement or purpose (*I am going to work to do my job*)
  TOO: in addition (*I'm coming too*)
  TWO: more than one; dual (*two officers patrol this area together*)

- **WEAR**: to put on (*I'll wear my new dress.*)
  WHERE: to question about place (*Where is the door?*)

- **YOUR**: belonging to you (*your car*)
  YOU'RE: you are (*you're going to need a new car*)

Commonly Confused Words

Some words are similar in meaning, but not synonyms. However, they are commonly confused in writing and speech. A hallmark of good writing is the proper use of these words.

Table 1.8 contains some commonly confused words.

Table 1.8. Commonly Confused Words

CONFUSED WORDS	DEFINITION
Amount	describes a noncountable quantity (*an unknown amount of jewelry was stolen*)
Number	describes a countable quantity (*an unknown number of necklaces was stolen*)
Bring	toward the speaker (*bring to me*)
Take	away from the speaker (*take away from me*)
Farther	a measurable distance (*the house farther up the road*)
Further	more or greater (*explain further what you mean*)
Fewer	a smaller amount of something plural (*fewer chairs*)
Less	a smaller amount of something that cannot be counted (*less water*)
Lose	to fail to win; to not be able to find something (*to lose a game; to lose one's keys*)
Loose	relaxed; not firmly in place (*my pants are loose*)

Special Spelling Rules

i comes before *e* except after *c*

Generally, the letter *i* comes before the letter *e* in a word except when the *i* is preceded by the letter *c*.

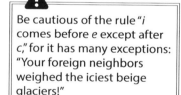

Be cautious of the rule "*i* comes before *e* except after *c*," for it has many exceptions: "Your foreign neighbors weighed the iciest beige glaciers!"

- p<u>ie</u>ce
- sal<u>ie</u>nt
- c<u>ei</u>ling
- con<u>ce</u>ivable

There are some notable exceptions where the letter e comes before the letter i, such as:

- words that end in–*cie*, like *proficient* or *ancient*
- plural words ending in –*cies*, like *policies*
- words with an *ay* sound, like *eight*, *vein*, or *neighbor*

When adding a suffix to a word, change the final *y* to an *i*.

- lazy → laziest
- tidy → tidily

For words that end with the letters –*le*, replace the letter *e* with the letter *y*: subtle → subtly

Plurals

Regular nouns are made plural by adding *s*. Irregular nouns can follow many different rules for pluralization, which are summarized in the table below.

Table 1.9. Irregular Plural Nouns

ENDS WITH . . .	MAKE IT PLURAL BY . . .	EXAMPLE
y	changing *y* to *i* and adding –*es*	baby → babies
f	changing *f* to *v* and adding –*es*	leaf → leaves
fe	changing *f* to *v* and adding –*s*	knife → knives
o	adding –*es*	potato → potatoes
us	changing –*us* to –*i*	nucleus → nuclei

ALWAYS THE SAME	DOESN'T FOLLOW THE RULES
sheep	man → men
deer	child → children
fish	person → people
moose	tooth → teeth
pants	goose → geese
binoculars	mouse → mice
scissors	ox → oxen

Pluralize words ending in –*ch, –s, –sh, –x,* or –*z* by adding –*es* to the end.

- catch → catches
- pass → passes
- push → pushes
- annex → annexes
- blitz → blitzes

An exception to the –*ch* rule includes words where the *ch* makes a *k* sound. For those words, simply add the letter *s* to the end of the word: stomach → stomachs.

Possessives Versus Contractions

A CONTRACTION is a combination of two words that is shortened by using an apostrophe to indicate the missing letter or letters. For instance, *cannot* is shortened to *can't*; the apostrophe stands in for the missing letters *n* and *o*.

A POSSESSIVE is a word with an apostrophe added to indicate possession. For example, rather than writing "the duty belt that belongs to Pat," write "Pat's duty belt."

A notable exception to this rule—and a common mistake—is the improper use of the contraction *it's* as a possessive, *its*.

The contraction for *it is* or *it has* is *it's*: "It's dangerous in that area of town at night."

The word *its* is possessive and shows ownership of the pronoun *it*, such as "the jury reached *its* verdict" or "the suspect's car was badly damaged, and *its* license plate was obscured."

Conjugating Verbs

The suffixes *–ed* or *–ing* added to a regular verb generally signify the verb's tense. For example, the present tense of the verb *to question* is *question* ("You question the suspect while I write the report.")

To show that the event happened in the past (or to form the past tense), the word *question* becomes *questioned*. And to refer to an action that is still happening (or to form the present participle), *question* becomes *questioning*. (See above for more details on conjugating verbs.)

There are some exceptions to the general rules for conjugating regular verbs.

For verbs ending with a silent *–e*, drop the *–e* before adding *–ed* or *–ing*.

- fake → faked → faking
- ache → ached → aching

When verbs end in the letters *–ee,* do not drop the second e. Instead, simply add *–d* or *–ing*.

- free → freed → freeing
- agree → agreed → agreeing

When the verb ends with a single vowel plus a consonant, and the stress is at the end of the word, then the consonant must be doubled before adding *–ed* or *–ing*.

- commit → committed → committing
- refer → referred → referring

If the stress is not at the end of the word, then the consonant can remain singular.

- target → targeted → targeting
- visit → visited → visiting

Verbs that end with the letter *c* must have the letter *k* added before receiving a suffix: panic → panicked → panicking

Examples

Read the following sentences and choose the correct spelling of the missing word.

21. The defendant asked the court to show him _____ in the punishment for his crime.

    (A) lienency
    (B) leniency
    (C) leneincy
    (D) leanency

22. Deputy Smith found _____ in the inmate's cell.
    (A) contriband
    (B) controband
    (C) contraband
    (D) contreband

23. Evidence that is fleeting or that can fade away over time is said to be of an _____ nature.
    (A) effervescent
    (B) evanecent
    (C) evanescent
    (D) evenescent

24. Officer Jones attempted to _____ the victim's blood loss by applying pressure to the wound.
    (A) mitagate
    (B) mitegate
    (C) midigate
    (D) mitigate

1. **(C) Correct.** *Minnesota* and *August* are proper nouns, and *coat* and *gloves* are common nouns. *I* is a pronoun, and *warm* is an adjective that modifies coat.

2. **(A) Correct.** *New* modifies the noun *chef*, and *boiling* modifies the noun *soup*.

   (B) Incorrect. *Carefully* is an adverb modifying the verb *stirred*.

   (C) Incorrect. *Heat* is a noun.

   (D) Incorrect. *Lowered* is a verb.

3. (A) Incorrect. *To* frequently indicates position; it does not make sense here.

   (B) Incorrect. *With* often implies a physical connection; it does not make sense here.

   (C) Correct. The correct preposition is *of*. The preposition *of* usually shows a relationship and may accompany a verb.

   (D) Incorrect. *About* is not idiomatically paired with *love* and is thus incorrect.

4. **(A) Correct.** Choice A should use quotation marks to set off a direct quote: *"I love apple pie!" John exclaimed with a smile.*

5. **(B) Correct.** The sentence is a question, so it should end with a question mark.

6. **(A) Correct.** The phrase is a prepositional phrase beginning with the preposition *with*. The preposition *with* modifies *the eager students*.

7. **(A) Correct.** In this sentence, the conjunction is joining together two contrasting ideas, so the correct answer is *but*.

8. (A) Incorrect. In this sentence, *hats* and *shoes* and *them* are all plural; they agree.

   (B) Correct. *The members of the band* is plural (*members*), so it should be replaced by the plural pronoun *their* instead of the singular *her*.

   (C) Incorrect. *Janitor* is singular, so the singular pronouns *his or her* are correct.

   (D) Incorrect. *You* and *you* agree in person and number. Note here that the pronoun *them* agrees with the antecedent *someone*. This is generally accepted usage, but it is unlikely to appear on an exam.

9. **(B) Correct.** Choice A contains a vague reference; it is unclear who was shot.

10. **(B) Correct.** This sentence contains a verb error; the verb is should be plural: are. All plural indefinite pronouns agree with plural verbs. Here, the subject of the sentence, *some*, is a plural indefinite pronoun, so it requires a plural verb.

11. **(A) Correct.** The phrase *by this time tomorrow* describes an action that will take place and be completed in the future, so the future perfect tense (*will have arrived*) should be used.

12. **(D) Correct.** This sentence should read, "Of the four speeches, Jerry's was the longest." The word *long* has only one syllable, so it should be modified with the suffix *–est*, not the word *most*.

13. **(A) Correct.** Choice B has a misplaced modifier (the word *often*).

14. **(A) Correct.** Choice B contains a sentence fragment.

15. **(B)** **Correct.** Choice A is a run-on sentence.

16. (A) Incorrect. *Inactive* means *dormant*.

    (B) **Correct.** *Unsettled* means *outstanding* or *due*.

    (C) Incorrect. *Unconfirmed* means *unsupported* or *uncorroborated*.

    (D) Incorrect. *Confirmed* means *verified*.

17. (A) Incorrect. *Confident* means *sure* or *secure*.

    (B) Incorrect. *Unsafe* means *dangerous* or *risky*.

    (C) **Correct.** *Self-satisfied* means *complacent*.

    (D) Incorrect. *Cheerful* means *pleasant* or *happy*.

18. (A) Incorrect. *Affirmed* means *to maintain as true* or *confirm*.

    (B) **Correct.** *Rescinded* means *recant*.

    (C) Incorrect. *Retold* means *told over again in a new way*.

    (D) Incorrect. *Regretted* means *felt remorse for*.

19. **(A)** **Correct.** *Trustworthy* means *credible*.

    (B) Incorrect. *Likeable* means *easy to like*.

    (C) Incorrect. *Suitable* means *appropriate*.

    (D) Incorrect. *Useful* means *being of use*.

20. (A) Incorrect. *Falsities* means *lies*.

    (B) Incorrect. *Inaccuracies* means *errors* or *mistakes*.

    (C) Incorrect. *Deception* means *ruse* or *trick*.

    (D) **Correct.** *Inconsistencies* means *discrepancies*.

21. **(B)** **Correct.** *Leniency* is the correct spelling.

22. **(C)** **Correct.** *Contraband* is the correct spelling.

23. **(C)** **Correct.** *Evanescent* is the correct spelling.

24. **(D)** **Correct.** *Mitigate* is the correct spelling.

2

READING COMPREHENSION

In the land of movies and television, law enforcement officers are rarely shown reading. Dirty Harry, John McClane, Horatio Caine, or Andy Sipowicz would be hard-pressed to pick up the penal code, case notes, or even a newspaper! But in the real world, where shooting up the entire downtown area; costing the city and county millions of dollars in repair costs and civil suits; and turning your back on suspects to don sunglasses can get you fired, sued, or hurt, reading is a huge part of the job.

Law enforcement officers spend a considerable amount of time reading reports, case law, statutes, subpoenas, warrants, investigative notes, memos and policy changes, news reports about policing and the community, and more. Understanding what you read is paramount because it may dictate how you do the job.

You do not need to use outside knowledge on reading comprehension questions. Remember, the answer is located within the passage.

Misunderstanding what you read could cost you your job. Reading comprehension is one of the most important aspects of law enforcement. The PELLETB tests applicants' reading comprehension abilities by presenting a passage to read, then asking several questions about the passage's content. The following information provides tips and tricks to improve your skills and navigate the reading comprehension section of the exam.

Reading for Understanding

Reading for understanding is different from reading for entertainment. Rather than simply skimming a passage for generalized information, the reader must dig more deeply into the text, make inferences and connections, and evaluate and interpret ideas and information. However, an integral part of reading comprehension is answering questions about the information. To be proficient at comprehension, readers must master several tasks while reading a particular passage:

DIFFERENTIATE FACT FROM OPINION. Many readers cannot tell the difference between fact and opinion. Contrary to popular belief, fact and opinion are not opposites; instead, they are differing types of statements. A **FACT** is a statement that can be proven by direct or objective evidence. Juries are called the "finders of fact" because they use the evidence presented to prove a statement. On the other hand, an OPINION, though it may be based in fact, is a statement established using belief or judgment and cannot be objectively proven true or false. Opinions are not necessarily wrong; they simply are not fact.

> Law enforcement officers often summarize in conversations. To ensure understanding, officers may repeat, in their own words, information a victim or suspect provides. The victim or suspect generally confirms or adjusts the restated information. To practice summarizing, after reading, take the information that is most important and restate it in it your own words.

DISTINGUISH BETWEEN WHAT IS IMPORTANT AND WHAT IS SIMPLY INTERESTING. When determining what is important in a passage, think about the main point and tone. What is the author trying to say? What is the main point? Information that tends to strengthen or weaken the main point is important. Information that does not strengthen or weaken the main point is simply interesting.

DETERMINE CAUSE-AND-EFFECT RELATIONSHIPS. Determine if there is a cause-and-effect relationship between pieces of information contained in the passage. Determining cause-and-effect relationships is important in comprehension as well as in establishing potential outcomes.

Look for words that show causal relationships, such as *because, since, therefore, thus,* and *so*.

COMPARE AND CONTRAST IDEAS AND INFORMATION. Connecting words often indicate transition within a passage. Understanding transitions can help keep you on track with the author's main point, rather than confusing you with opposing points of view in the passage. Look for words that show a shift in the author's position, such as *however, but, rather, in contrast,* and *although*.

DRAW CONCLUSIONS. Law enforcement officers regularly make inferences, draw conclusions, and make determinations based on information presented. After reading the passage, ask yourself:

- What judgments can be made based on the information provided?
- What evidence included in the passage supports that judgment?
- Are there other interpretations that can be made using the provided information and evidence?

Question Types

Reading comprehension tests generally use seven basic question types. They are explored in more detail in the chapter.

> Read the passage carefully. Do not skim the passage. Read it two or three times to ensure you understand what the passage is communicating. Remember, this section is examining comprehension. Reading too quickly can cause you to miss important information.

1. **WHAT'S THE MAIN POINT?** These questions ask you to identify the author's thesis or hypothesis. A question stem relating to this question type might ask, "The passage was primarily concerned with which of the following?" Check the thesis statement or conclusion for the answer to these types of questions.

2. **WHAT'S THE SUPPORTING IDEA?** These questions generally ask you to locate specific information. A

question stem relating to this question type might ask, "The passage mentions each of the following EXCEPT…" You may need to reread the passage to find the answer. You might look for keywords in the answer choices to help steer you in the right direction.

3. **DRAWING INFERENCES.** Questions that require you to draw inferences often ask, "The passage implies which of the following?" The answer choices generally will closely imitate the text of the passage and rely upon specific facts provided.

4. **WHAT'S THE TONE?** These questions ask you to identify the author's attitude. Question stems generally ask, "The author's tone is best described as…"

5. **APPLY THE THEME TO OTHER CIRCUMSTANCES.** Questions requiring you to apply information from the passage to a similar situation often take the following form: "The author would most likely agree with which of the following?" There is no shortcut or trick to answering these question types. The key is identifying the heart of the passage and relating it to similar answer choices.

6. **LOGICAL REASONING.** This question style is the reverse of the "Application" question style. Logical reasoning questions ask you to take information from *outside* the passage and apply it to the passage to make determinations. An example of a logical reasoning question might be "Which of the following, if true, would most weaken the main point of the second paragraph?" Understanding the author's main point or argument and using your reasoning abilities to determine the value of answer choices will help you answer these questions.

> ⚠️
> Read the passage before the question. Reading the question first can distract you from the main point of the passage. An error is more likely if you answer the question prematurely and without full understanding.

7. **RELATING DIFFERENT IDEAS.** These questions require you to determine the relationship between different ideas or parts of the passage. Questions are framed in a variety of ways, but they might ask how two paragraphs relate to each other or how an idea in one sentence contrasts with an idea later in the passage.

TOPIC AND MAIN IDEA

The **TOPIC** is a word or short phrase that explains what a passage is about. The **MAIN IDEA** is a complete sentence that explains what the author is trying to say about the topic. Generally, the **TOPIC SENTENCE** is the first (or near the first) sentence in a paragraph. It is a general statement that introduces the topic so the reader knows what to expect.

> ✓
> To find the main idea, identify the topic and then ask, *What is the author trying to tell me about the topic?*

The **SUMMARY SENTENCE**, on the other hand, frequently (but not always!) comes at the end of a paragraph or passage because it wraps up all the ideas presented. This sentence summarizes what an author has said about the topic. Some passages, particularly short ones, will not include a summary sentence.

Table 2.1. Identifying Topic and Main Idea

Noise complaints are one of the most common calls received by police officers in cities and suburban areas. Close quarters and strong personalities make it more likely that neighbors will butt heads; the officer's job is to keep the peace. Usually, an officer can solve the problem by warning the offender. Most people will immediately turn down their music or end a late-night party when they find out they risk a hefty fine. On rare occasions, officers will issue citations for violating city ordinances or will arrest offenders for crimes like disorderly conduct.

TOPIC SENTENCE	Noise complaints are one of the most common calls received by police officers in cities and suburban areas.
TOPIC	noise complaints
SUMMARY SENTENCE	Close quarters and strong personalities make it more likely that neighbors will butt heads; the officer's job is to keep the peace.
MAIN IDEA	Officers respond to noise complaints, which are very common in crowded areas, to restore order.

Examples

1. **Topic**

   Police dogs usually work from six to nine years. K-9 officers have a variety of professional responsibilities: sniffing out explosives and narcotics, finding missing persons and human remains, and protecting officers. Many of them retire to live a comfortable life with their handlers, who know them better than anyone.

   What is the topic of the passage?

   (A) dog lifespan

   (B) police dogs

   (C) dog handlers

   (D) canine retirement

2. **Main Idea**

   The Battle of the Little Bighorn, commonly called Custer's Last Stand, was a battle between the Seventh Cavalry Regiment of the US Army and the combined forces of the Lakota, the Northern Cheyenne, and the Arapaho tribes. Led by war leaders Crazy Horse and Chief Gall and religious leader Sitting Bull, the allied tribes of the Plains Indians decisively defeated their US foes. Two hundred and sixty-eight US soldiers were killed, including Lieutenant Colonel George Armstrong Custer, two of his brothers, his nephew, his brother-in-law, and six Indian scouts.

   What is the main idea of this passage?

   (A) Most of Custer's family died in the Battle of the Little Bighorn.

   (B) The Seventh Cavalry Regiment was formed to fight Native American tribes.

   (C) Sitting Bull and George Custer were fierce enemies.

   (D) The Battle of the Little Bighorn was a significant victory for the Plains Indians.

SUPPORTING DETAILS

Statements that describe or explain the main idea are **SUPPORTING DETAILS**. Supporting details are often found after the topic sentence. They support the main idea through examples, descriptions, and explanations.

Authors may add details to support their argument or claim. **FACTS** are details that point to truths, while **OPINIONS** are based on personal beliefs or judgments. To differentiate between fact and opinion, look for statements that express feelings, attitudes, or beliefs that cannot be proven (opinions) and statements that can be proven (facts).

> To find supporting details, look for sentences that connect to the main idea and tell more about it.

Table 2.2. Supporting Details and Fact and Opinion

Police academies have strict physical requirements for cadets. Cadets must pass fitness tests and train daily. As a result, some new recruits worry about their physical fitness before heading into the academy. Some graduates suggest focusing on core strength. Others believe that boxing is the best workout. We feel that cardiovascular activity is the most important exercise.

SUPPORTING DETAILS	Cadets must pass fitness tests and train daily.
FACT	Police academies have strict physical requirements for cadets.
OPINION	We feel that cardiovascular activity is the most important exercise.

Examples

3. **Supporting Details**

   Increasingly, companies are turning to subcontracting services rather than hiring full-time employees. This provides companies with advantages like greater flexibility, reduced legal responsibility to employees, and lower possibility of unionization within the company. However, this has led to increasing confusion and uncertainty over the legal definition of employment. Courts have grappled with questions about the hiring company's responsibility in maintaining fair labor practices. Companies argue that they delegate that authority to subcontractors, while unions and other worker advocate groups argue that companies still have a legal obligation to the workers who contribute to their business.

   Which detail BEST supports the idea that contracting employees is beneficial to companies?

   (A) Uncertainty over the legal definition of employment increases.

   (B) Companies still have a legal obligation to contractors.

   (C) There is a lower possibility of unionization within the company.

   (D) Contractors, not companies, control fair labor practices.

4. **Fact and Opinion**

   An officer cited a motorist for reckless driving. The driver was performing unsafe maneuvers. The motorist was "doing donuts," rotating the vehicle. The officer observed this activity in a parking lot after dark. The officer wrote a citation. In addition, the vehicle was impounded.

Which statement from the passage is an opinion?

(A) An officer cited a motorist for reckless driving.

(B) The driver was performing unsafe maneuvers.

(C) The motorist was "doing donuts," rotating the vehicle.

(D) In addition, the vehicle was impounded.

DRAWING CONCLUSIONS

Look for facts, character actions and dialogue, how each sentence connects to the topic, and the author's reasoning for an argument when drawing conclusions.

Readers can use information that is EXPLICIT, or clearly stated, along with information that is IMPLICIT, or indirect, to make inferences and DRAW CONCLUSIONS. Readers can determine meaning from what is implied by using details, context clues, and prior knowledge. When answering questions, consider what is known from personal experiences and make note of all information the author has provided before drawing a conclusion.

Table 2.3. Drawing Conclusions

When the Spanish-American War broke out in 1898, the US Army was small and understaffed. President William McKinley called for 1,250 volunteers to serve in the First US Volunteer Cavalry. The ranks were quickly filled by cowboys, gold prospectors, hunters, gamblers, Native Americans, veterans, police officers, and college students looking for an adventure. The officer corps was composed of veterans of previous wars. With more volunteers than it could accept, the army set high standards: all the recruits had to be skilled on horseback and with guns. Consequently, they became known as the Rough Riders.

QUESTION	Why are the volunteers named Rough Riders?
EXPLICIT INFORMATION	Different people volunteered, men were looking for adventure, recruits had to be extremely skilled on horseback and with guns due to a glut of volunteers.
IMPLICIT INFORMATION	Men had previous occupations; officer corps veterans worked with volunteers.
CONCLUSION DRAWN	The men were called Rough Riders because they were inexperienced yet enthusiastic to help with the war and were willing to put in extra effort to join.

Example

5. Drawing Conclusions

"Swatting" is a dangerous practice. Someone falsely reports a crime in progress at a location to attract a large number of police to the site. The false crime usually involves hostages or a similar violent scenario, so police are prepared for confrontation. In fact, the term swatting is derived from the name for those police who specialize in such situations: the SWAT team, which carries high-caliber weapons and deploys flash bangs and tear gas. In a swatting incident, innocent citizens are shocked by a sudden police raid on their home. Likewise, police ready to face a violent perpetrator are surprised to find a family eating dinner or watching TV. The confusion caused by the false information and urgency of the raid make it very dangerous for all involved. Tragic outcomes are not uncommon.

Which conclusion about the effects of swatting is most likely true?

(A) Swatting is increasingly common, thanks to social media.

(B) Swatting mostly occurs where there are large SWAT teams.

(C) Swatting is usually harmless, though a waste of police time.

(D) Swatting can result in injury or death to innocent citizens or officers.

THE AUTHOR'S PURPOSE AND POINT OF VIEW

The **AUTHOR'S PURPOSE** is his or her reason for writing a text. Authors may write to share an experience, to entertain, to persuade, or to inform readers. This can be done through persuasive, expository, and narrative writing.

PERSUASIVE WRITING influences the actions and thoughts of readers. Authors state an opinion, then provide reasons that support the opinion. **EXPOSITORY WRITING** outlines and explains steps in a process. Authors focus on a sequence of events. **NARRATIVE WRITING** tells a story. Authors include a setting, plot, characters, problem, and solution in the text.

 Use the acronym P.I.E.S.— *persuade, inform, entertain, state*—to help you remember elements of an author's purpose.

Authors also share their **POINT OF VIEW** (perspectives, attitudes, and beliefs) with readers. Identify the author's point of view by word choice, details, descriptions, and characters' actions. The author's attitude, or **TONE**, can be found in word choice that conveys feelings or stance on a topic.

TEXT STRUCTURE is the way the author organizes a text. A text can be organized to show problem and solution, comparison and contrast, or even cause and effect. Structure of a text can give insight into an author's purpose and point of view. If a text is organized to pose an argument or advertise a product, it can be considered persuasive. The author's point of view will be revealed in how thoughts and opinions are expressed in the text.

Table 2.4. The Author's Purpose and Point of View

Officer ride-alongs are a great way for community members to get to know law enforcement officers. They are a valuable opportunity for students, journalists, community leaders, and those considering a career in law enforcement to learn more about the day-to-day experiences of police business. In a ride-along, you join an officer as he or she responds to calls, stops cars, and interacts with the public. Riders can ask questions and see the world from the perspective of a cop. Ride-alongs are a wonderful way for members of the public to learn about policing.

AUTHOR'S PURPOSE	persuade readers of the benefit of ride-alongs
POINT OF VIEW	advocates ride-alongs as "a great way for community members to get to know law enforcement officers"
TONE	positive, encouraging, pointing out the benefits of ride-alongs, using positive words like *great* and *wonderful*
STRUCTURE	descriptive: describes ride-alongs, giving specific examples to support the argument that they are valuable

Examples

6. Author's Purpose

Several law enforcement departments in the United States have implemented sUAS (small unmanned aircraft systems), or drone programs. Drones provide intelligence, surveillance, and reconnaissance, known as ISR, helping inform decision-makers in reconstructing accidents and crime scenes, finding victims in search and rescue, and managing fire scenes. Local jurisdictions, such as the Los Angeles County Sheriff's Department, use drones. So do federal agencies like the US Border Patrol. What was once a military tool is becoming a valuable resource for law enforcement.

What is the purpose of this passage?

(A) to argue that drones are important for patrol

(B) to explain the history of drones in law enforcement

(C) to persuade readers that drone programs should be funded

(D) to describe how drones are used by law enforcement agencies

7. Point of View

Any law enforcement officer should expect to use force on the job at some point. Fortunately, officers have many nonlethal options for controlling a suspect or situation. Tasers, pepper spray, and batons are all effective for neutralizing a threat in many circumstances. Officers also train in basic ground and hand-to-hand tactics, though if possible they should avoid physical encounters for safety reasons. However, in certain situations officers must use their service pistols, which may result in a fatality.

Which of the following BEST describes what the author believes?

(A) Most forms of nonlethal force are effective, but not all.

(B) Lethal force should never be used because it is unethical.

(C) Officers should use nonlethal force if possible.

(D) Physical encounters should always be avoided.

8. Tone

Managing people is complicated in any field, and law enforcement is no different. Managers must balance administrative, financial, disciplinary, and policy responsibilities. Good managers also need to be aware of their subordinates' mental health in stressful fields like law enforcement. Recognizing the signs of stress, depression, substance abuse, and afflictions like post-traumatic stress disorder (PTSD) is an important skill for those who manage law enforcement personnel. The department can provide officers with support for mental wellness, improving their job performance and safety. The sooner a supervisor can spot symptoms, the faster the officer can receive assistance.

Which of the following best describes the author's attitude toward officers' mental health?

(A) dismissive

(B) sympathetic

(C) pitying

(D) angry

9. Text Structure

Increasingly, police departments require law enforcement officers to wear body cameras when they interact with members of the public. Some officers agree with this policy because the cameras provide protection against false complaints of police misconduct. Footage can exonerate police officers, proving their professionalism in situations. Other officers are cautious, worried that the cameras could limit officer discretion. Their concern is that supervisors might review and second-guess the officers' decisions during a call. What is undeniable is that the trend of body cameras is not going away as more jurisdictions across America adopt them.

What is the structure of this text?

(A) cause and effect

(B) order and sequence

(C) problem and solution

(D) compare and contrast

COMPARING PASSAGES

Sometimes readers need to compare and contrast two texts. After reading and identifying the main idea of each text, look for similarities and differences in the main idea, details, claims, evidence, characters, and so on.

When answering questions about two texts, first identify whether the question is about a similarity or a difference. Then look for specific details in the text that connect to the answers. After that, determine which answer choice best describes the similarity or difference.

> ⚠ Use a Venn diagram, table, or highlighters to organize similarities and differences between texts.

Table 2.5. Comparing Passages

INTRANASALLY ADMINISTERED NALOXONE

Because even tiny amounts of the dangerous narcotic Fentanyl can result in overdose or death, many law enforcement officers carry the anti-overdose drug naloxone in case they encounter the frequently abused substance. Naloxone can be administered intranasally, allowing for rapid absorption into the bloodstream. The rescuer lays the victim on his or her back and sprays the medication into one nostril. The rescuer needs minimal training to administer naloxone in this way.

INJECTABLE NALOXONE

Naloxone, a medication that counteracts opioid overdose, is carried by many law enforcement officers in case of accidental contact with powerful narcotics like Fentanyl. Naloxone must be injected by trained first responders. Injectable naloxone is effective when the nasal cavity is damaged, for instance, if the victim has head trauma. Injectable naloxone is also used on detection dogs that have accidentally inhaled Fentanyl or another opioid and need a lower dose of naloxone than a human would.

SIMILARITIES (COMPARISON)	Both substances are used by law enforcement to fight accidental opioid overdose.
DIFFERENCES (CONTRAST)	Intranasally administered naloxone works rapidly and can be given by anyone. Injectable naloxone must be administered by a trained first responder and is more effective in specific situations.

Example

10. Comparing Passages

Self-Driving Cars: A Safer America

Self-driving cars, already present on our streets, are the wave of the future. They will make roads safer. Unlike human drivers, self-driving cars don't drink and drive, get lost in conversation, or fumble with phones. They can also be programmed to strictly adhere to the speed limit and traffic laws. That makes them the best bet for road and highway safety. Law enforcement officials will have more time to pursue violent criminals if they don't need to spend as much time monitoring highways for speeders and unsafe drivers.

The Dangers of Autonomous Vehicles

Many people are excited about autonomous vehicles, or self-driving cars, but they are risky machines. Already, several have been involved in deadly accidents, failing to brake for pedestrians or making inappropriate turns resulting in wrecks. Autonomous vehicles can malfunction; they occupy a gray area for law enforcement. What if an autonomous vehicle is speeding? How can highway patrol pull it over? What is the role for the traffic officer in an accident caused by a self-driving car? Who is accountable? There is no substitution for an experienced human driver with good judgment.

Which of these statements BEST compares the information in both texts?

(A) Autonomous vehicles are a social advantage.

(B) People are already using self-driving cars.

(C) Self-driving cars occupy a legal gray area.

(D) Officers will benefit from self-driving cars.

MEANING OF WORDS

To understand the meanings of unfamiliar words, use **CONTEXT CLUES**. Context clues are hints the author provides to help readers define difficult words. They can be found in words or phrases in the same sentence or in a neighboring sentence. Look for synonyms, antonyms, definitions, examples, and explanations in the text to determine the meaning of the unfamiliar word.

Sometimes parts of a word can make its meaning easier to determine. **AFFIXES** are added to **ROOT WORDS** (a word's basic form) to modify meaning. **PREFIXES** are added to the beginning of root words, while **SUFFIXES** are added to the ending. Divide words into parts, finding meaning in each part. Take, for example, the word *unjustifiable*: the prefix is *un–* (*not*), the root word is *justify* ("to prove reasonable"), and the suffix is *–able* (referring to a quality). Affixes are discussed in more detail in chapter 1.

> ⚠
> Use what you know about a word to figure out its meaning, then look for clues in the sentence or paragraph.

Another way to determine the meaning of unknown words is to consider their denotation and connotation with other words in the sentence. **DENOTATION** is the literal meaning of a word, while **CONNOTATION** is the positive or negative associations of a word.

Authors use words to convey thoughts, but the meaning may be different from a literal meaning of the words. This is called **FIGURATIVE LANGUAGE**. Types of figurative language include similes, metaphors, hyperboles, and personification.

Similes compare two things that are not alike with the words *like* or *as*. Metaphors are used to compare two things that are not exactly alike but may share a certain characteristic.

Hyperboles are statements that exaggerate something to make a point or to draw attention to a certain feature. Personification involves using human characteristics to describe an animal or object.

Table 2.6. Meanings of Words

Check fraud used to be a major crime, but today fewer people than ever use paper checks. Still, criminals continue to find ways to steal from consumers. Identity theft is a threat to all Americans as more people use credit cards and electronic financial applications than cash. Despite <u>encryption</u> techniques that protect personal details, computer hackers periodically uncover consumers' financial information in security breaches. Small-time thieves steal credit cards, use card skimmers at gas stations, or make fake cards with specialized machines.

CONTEXT CLUES	Techniques *protect* personal details; the details are still *uncovered* for criminal use.
AFFIXES	The prefix *en–* in *encryption* means *cause to*. The suffix *–ion* suggests an act or process.
ROOTS	The root of the word *encryption* is *crypt*, which means *hide* or *conceal*.
MEANING	*Encryption* means "the process of causing something to be hidden."

Examples

11. **Context Clues**

    After a few high-profile missing-persons cases in the 1970s and 1980s, parents in many communities became concerned about "stranger danger." Families worried that their children would be <u>abducted</u>, taken by criminal outsiders. However, when a child goes missing, the perpetrator is usually someone the child knows. Family members make up the majority of perpetrators in cases of missing children. It is very rare that a child is kidnapped by a total stranger, though it can happen.

    What does *abducted* mean as it is used in the passage?

    (A) taken by criminal outsiders

    (B) the perpetrator

    (C) family members make up

    (D) "stranger danger"

12. **Root Words and Affixes**

    Unfortunately, automobile accidents happen. The good news is, most result in only minor damage to vehicles. Still, drivers are responsible for calling the police and reporting the incident, regardless of its severity. An officer will arrive to take the statement of each driver and survey the scene. The officer will closely examine the drivers' behavior and mannerisms to determine if their claims are <u>credible</u>. After all the evidence is collected, reviewed, and approved, the insurance company assigns blame to one party. The officer's role is key in this determination.

    Based on affixes and context clues, what does *credible* mean?

    (A) believable

    (B) achievable

    (C) likeable

    (D) noticeable

13. Figurative Language

Nothing in the world is harder than waking up for a job you don't love. Who wants to drag themselves to work every day? That's why it's important to follow your passions. Many say that serving the public in law enforcement is more than just a job; it's a calling. Police officers risk their lives to serve and protect the public. It takes a certain kind of person to thrive in law enforcement.

Which type of figurative language is used in the second sentence?

(A) simile

(B) metaphor

(C) personification

(D) hyperbole

1. **(B) Correct.** The topic of the passage is police dogs. The passage mentions how long they work, their handlers, and the usual retirement circumstances of police dogs as supporting ideas.

2. **(D) Correct.** The author writes that "the allied tribes...decisively defeated their US foes," and the remainder of the passage provides details to support this idea.

3. **(C) Correct.** The passage specifically presents this detail as one of the advantages of subcontracting services.

4. **(B) Correct.** The statement "The driver was performing unsafe maneuvers" is a judgment about the safety of the actions taken by the driver. The driver (or his attorney) might argue that his driving was safe.

5. **(D) Correct.** The passage states that swatting is dangerous because of confusion caused by false information and the nature of a violent raid. The sentence "Tragic outcomes are not uncommon" suggests that injury or death can happen.

6. **(D) Correct.** The text provides details on how drones are used and what departments use them.

7. **(C) Correct.** The author discusses many options for nonlethal force, using the word *fortunately* to show a preference for it. However, the author also allows that lethal force is sometimes necessary.

8. **(B) Correct.** The author states that "[t]he department can provide officers with support" and that supervisors should "be aware of their subordinates' mental health." By taking these positions, the author is being sympathetic and supportive of officers' mental health.

9. **(D) Correct.** In this text, two perspectives on body cameras are compared and contrasted.

10. **(B) Correct.** Both passages indicate that self-driving cars, or autonomous vehicles, are already in use.

11. **(A) Correct.** The phrase "taken by criminal outsiders" redefines the word *abducted* in the sentence.

12. **(A) Correct.** The root *cred* means *believe*. The words *evidence*, *reviewed*, and *approved* are context clues hinting that something needs to be believed and accepted.

13. **(B) Correct.** The writer uses the metaphor *drag*. No one literally drags himself or herself to work.

3

CLOZE

The CLOZE test measures reading comprehension by testing how easy it is for a target audience to read and understand a particular passage. It also measures vocabulary and knowledge of the subject on which the passage is based. Testtakers are provided a passage to read. The first and last sentences remain intact, and then every seventh word in the passage is deleted and replaced with the same number of blanks as letters in that word. The test requires applicants to provide the missing words using context, deduction, and reasoning in order to show that they understand the passage. In many cases, more than one word may fit in a blank space and be considered a correct answer. However, all answers must fit the word length indicated in the passage.

Most people find that studying for the CLOZE test is the most difficult section of the PELLETB. However, reasoning and common sense can help you find the answers to this portion of the exam. The following chapter can help you develop a strategy for tackling the CLOZE.

PLAYING HANGMAN

Have you ever played the game Hangman? As part of the game, your opponent draws a stick-figure picture of a gallows above a set of dashes, which correspond to the letters that compose the words or phrase your opponent is thinking of. You can guess any letter in an attempt to fill in the blank dashes with correct letters that make up the missing word. If you guess correctly, your opponent fills in one of the blanks with that letter, providing a clue to the word or phrase. If you guess incorrectly, your opponent will draw a piece of a stick figure onto the gallows. The goal is to guess the entire word or phrase before the stick figure is complete.

THE CLOZE CAN BE FUN!

i r m l

Figure 3.1. Hangman!

Playing Hangman is a fun way for children to challenge each other mentally. The CLOZE test is like a game of Hangman for adults. It has blank lines and clues, and it challenges your mental sharpness. In the next section, we provide several tips to help you succeed on the CLOZE.

TACKLING THE CLOZE

Careful Reading

A key strategy for tackling the CLOZE section of the PELLETB is to read the passage slowly and with care. Because the CLOZE tests reading comprehension, you will need to consider the meaning of each individual word, as well as the sentence in which those words appear. Before you begin answering questions, you should follow the steps below:

READ THROUGH THE ENTIRE PASSAGE. This step may seem obvious, but as you read, you will want to scan the passage for important names and figures and skim for general meaning and context. Circle any sentences that you do not understand, and underline sections that seem particularly important. You might be surprised by what your brain "sees" as you read the passage for the first time. Do not be afraid to take notes in the margins of your test booklet.

SUMMARIZE THE PASSAGE. After you read the selection, make sure you understand the basics of the passage, such as the topic, the main idea, and the conclusion. The topic is a word or short phrase describing the subject of the passage, and the main idea develops the topic throughout the paragraph using details or concrete examples. The conclusion is how the author wraps up his or her argument. By quickly identifying these individual parts, you will be able to answer questions about the passage as a whole.

LOOK FOR REPETITION. If you see a noun repeated throughout the passage, that word is usually part of the main idea. Underline or circle it; it is likely to be the correct answer to at least one question.

Context Clues

CONTEXT CLUES are hints in the text. It is important to read the entire passage for context. However, the words immediately around sets of blanks will reveal details that can help you determine the precise letters and words you need to find the correct answer.

Read the sentences and phrases before and after the missing word very carefully. The preceding and following sentences and phrases often hold clues in grammar, phrasing, and mechanics.

Look for context clues like DEFINITIONS in the passage. Sometimes the text provides definitions of unknown words. Definitions might appear inside quotes or dashes. A definition following a set of blanks might reveal the correct word. Take a look at this example.

> The _ _ _ _ _ _, the person who sees the crime take place, should be interviewed.

The phrase "the person who sees the crime take place" defines the missing word that precedes it. The seven-letter word *witness* fits in the blanks and means exactly that—someone who sees something (such as a crime) occur.

Grammatical Aspects

Pay attention to VERB TENSE. Make note of past, present, and future tense, and make sure the answers use the same tense as the passage. Some missing words might be verbs or parts of verb phrases. You might be able to figure out the correct word, but the word you have in mind is too short or long for the set of blanks in question. A suffix relating to tense might make the difference.

When it comes to verbs, also pay attention to PREPOSITIONS. Many verbs take specific prepositions (*speak to*, *look at*, and so on). There is no real rule for these idiomatic expressions; you learned them as you learned to speak English. Let's explore the example below.

> The chief _ _ _ _ _ to the press earlier today. As he was speaking, he discussed several recent arrests.

In this example, the answer is *spoke*. The reader has two contextual hints about tense: the word *earlier* and the verb phrase *was speaking*. It is clear that whatever the chief did to the press, it happened in the past.

Another context clue in this example is the preposition *to*. Whatever precedes that preposition must make sense with it. *Spoke to* is an idiomatic expression; it would sound wrong and be incorrect to say, "The chief spoke *at* the press" or "The chief spoke *through* the press."

Pay attention to SINGULAR and PLURAL. Note whether preceding and successive words are singular or plural, and make sure your answers match.

> Five _ _ _ _ _ _ _ _ were arrested after witnesses reported seeing them break into the back of the store. One _ _ _ _ _ _ _ also saw a suspect standing watch outside the doors of the store.

It is clear that a plural word is needed for the first set of blanks, since the adjective *five* is used to describe it. Similarly, the second set of blanks must be singular, as it is modified by *one*. From the context, the reader can safely assume that five *suspects* were arrested. By the same logic, *witness* fits into the second set. And, from the context, it makes sense that a witness would see a suspect in the middle of committing a crime.

Transition Words

Passages on the CLOZE exam routinely include transition words and phrases. TRANSITION WORDS AND PHRASES connect different ideas within sentences or between paragraphs in a text. Because they lend order and structure to sentences and paragraphs, transition words aid in reading comprehension. Transition words are useful tools for deciphering the missing words in a CLOZE passage.

There are many different kinds of transition words. For example, passages may include transition words that suggest SIMILARITIES, like *and*, *in addition*, *similarly*, and *also*.

> She received a ticket for her expired registration; she **also** got a _ _ _ _ _ _ for not having a license.

In the example above, the word *also* connects the first clause with the second clause. The woman was ticketed for her expired registration, so it can be deduced that she received an additional *ticket* for not having a license.

Transition words can also suggest OPPOSITES. Look for words like *however, on the other hand, but, although,* and *conversely*.

> There seemed to be ample evidence in favor of the defendant; **however**, he was found _ _ _ _ _ _ at trial.

In the example, the word *however* signals to the reader that the following clause will have an opposite meaning to the idea that preceded it. With a lot of evidence in favor of the defendant, chances are he would be found not guilty, but the word *however* indicates the opposite. The word *guilty* fits in the set of blanks.

Missing words might even be transition words themselves. Check the context around the blanks to determine the meaning of the word.

> The officer **liked** his new partner, _ _ _ he **missed** his colleagues in his previous precinct.

In this example, the officer has mixed, or opposing, emotions. Chances are, a transition word indicating opposites—like the word *but*—makes sense here. He likes his new assigned partner, *but* he also misses his old colleagues. Grammatically, *but* also makes sense because it is connecting two independent clauses, using a comma after the word *partner*.

Use Outside Knowledge

Using basic outside knowledge to fill in the blanks is an appropriate tactic for the questions found on the CLOZE exam, unlike other portions of the PELLETB. You are allowed to GUESS THE MEANING OF SENTENCES OR WORDS BASED ON YOUR OWN KNOWLEDGE. For instance, a typical reader would know that the title of the leader of police at a station is the police CHIEF, that a local police jurisdiction is the PRECINCT, and so forth. This is one place on the PELLETB where your own outside knowledge can be beneficial.

> The people who saw the robbery take place were asked to be _ _ _ _ _ _ _ _ _ in court.
>
> The three women described the _ _ _ _ _ _ _ to the police after the robbery.

In the first example, the word *witnesses* fits the blank. Most testtakers will know that people who have seen a crime take place can be called as witnesses in court, so this is a safe guess. In the second example, the word *suspect* fits. The savvy testtaker can use his or her outside knowledge of police procedure to guess the suspect is whom the women would be describing.

Examples

1. **CLOZE Passage One**

A job in law enforcement involves much more than just arresting criminals. Officers must have good communication skills. _ _ _ _ also must have the ability to _ _ _ _ _ clear, accurate reports and to understand _ _ _ _ _ _ _ materials. Those wishing to become a _ _ _ enforcement officer should work on improving _ _ _ _ _ reading and writing skills prior to _ _ _ _ _ _ _ _ for the job. Brushing up on _ _ _ _ _ _ _ grammar, vocabulary, and spelling is a _ _ _ _ place to start. In addition, applicants _ _ _ _ _ _ also work on understanding context, which _ _ essential. Context is the setting of _ _ _ communication. The setting is created by _ _ _ _ _ that come immediately before or after _ given word or passage, which provide _ _ _ _ _ _ _.

Because the PELLETB is designed to _ _ _ _ a very specific group of people, _ _ _ _ _ _ _ _ _ _ should study reading comprehension and vocabulary _ _ _ _ _ _ _ to the law. Study guides focused _ _ the format of the PELLETB can _ _ _ _ applicants prepare for the exam. The more prepared an applicant is, the more likely he or she will be successful.

2. **CLOZE Passage Two**

Vandalism occurred in a quiet residential neighborhood. Two male suspects were arrested at _ _ _ Twin Oaks Apartments last night. The _ _ _ _ _ _, who responded to a call from _ _ _ of the residents, reported that the _ _ _ vandalized a door with cans of spray _ _ _ _ _ and damaged two large sliding-glass _ _ _ _ _ _ on the east side of the _ _ _ _ _ _ _ _. Drug paraphernalia was found in their _ _ _ _ _ _ _ _ _ _, along with a crowbar. There were no signs of breaking _ _ _ entering.

Police interviewed three witnesses at the _ _ _ _ _ of the crime. The first witness

_ _ _ _ _ _ _ _ _ _ the men in custody. The _ _ _ _ _ _ witness said he saw the men _ _ _ _ _ _ _ _ _ the door with spray paint. Additionally, _ _ _ witness saw the suspects damage the _ _ _ _ _ on the east side of the _ _ _ _ _ _ _ _ complex. A third witness reported seeing the _ _ _ men on the premises _ _ _ _ _ _ _ in the evening, around 7:00 p.m.

A hearing for the two suspects _ _ _ _ be held early next week. The _ _ _ are charged with trespassing and _ _ _ _ _ _ _ _ _ _ _ of property. A public defender will _ _ appointed to represent the men in court. Because of prior criminal records, they remain in custody.

ANSWER KEY

CLOZE Passage One

A job in law enforcement involves much more than just arresting criminals. Officers must have good communication skills. **T H E Y / C O P S** also must have the ability to **W R I T E** clear, accurate reports and to understand **W R I T T E N** materials. Those wishing to become a **L A W** enforcement officer should work on improving **T H E I R** reading and writing skills prior to **A P P L Y I N G** for the job. Brushing up on **E N G L I S H / W R I T T E N** grammar, vocabulary, and spelling is a **G O O D** place to start. In addition, applicants **S H O U L D** also work on understanding context, which **I S** essential. Context is the setting of **A L L** communication. The setting is created by **W O R D S** that come immediately before or after **A** given word or passage, which provide **C O N T E X T / C L A R I T Y**.

Because the PELLETB is designed to **T E S T** a very specific group of people, **A P P L I C A N T S** should study reading comprehension and vocabulary **R E L A T E D** to the law. Study guides focused **O N** the format of the PELLETB can **H E L P** applicants prepare for the exam. The more prepared an applicant is, the more likely he or she will be successful.

CLOZE Passage Two

Vandalism occurred in a quiet residential neighborhood. Two male suspects were arrested at **T H E** Twin Oaks Apartments last night. The **P O L I C E**, who responded to a call from **O N E** of the residents, reported that the **M E N** vandalized a door with cans of spray **P A I N T** and damaged two large sliding-glass **D O O R S** on the east side of the **B U I L D I N G**. Drug paraphernalia was found in their **P O S S E S S I O N**, along with a crowbar. There were no signs of breaking **A N D** entering.

Police interviewed three witnesses at the **S C E N E** of the crime. The first witness **I D E N T I F I E D** the men in custody. The **S E C O N D** witness said he saw the men **V A N D A L I Z E** the door with spray paint. Additionally, **T H E / O N E** witness saw the suspects damage the **D O O R S** on the east side of the **A P A R T M E N T** complex. A third witness reported seeing the **T W O** men on the premises **E A R L I E R** in the evening, around 7:00 p.m.

A hearing for the two suspects **W I L L** be held early next week. The **M E N** are charged with trespassing and **D E S T R U C T I O N** of property. A public defender will **B E** appointed to represent the men in court. Because of prior criminal records, they remain in custody.

PART II: PRACTICE

PRACTICE TEST ONE

WRITING

The writing test measures three aspects of good writing: clarity, vocabulary, and spelling.

CLARITY
In the following sentence pairs, identify the sentence that is most clearly written.

1.

A) Julie was happy to get back to her life after the trial she felt she received justice.

B) Julie was happy to get back to her life after the trial. She felt she received justice.

2.

A) Marge told Ruth that Marge's supervisor wanted to speak with Ruth.

B) Marge told Ruth that her supervisor wanted to speak with her.

3.

A) Kelly did not see the cyclist riding in her blind spot, and she hit him with her car as she made the right turn.

B) Kelly did not see the cyclist riding in her blind spot, and she hit him with her car. As she made the right turn.

4.

A) Officers who train rarely are caught off guard.

B) Officers who train are rarely caught off guard.

5.

A) The defendant was angry at the sentence he received. He antagonized the judge out of frustration.

B) The defendant was angry at the sentence he received he antagonized the judge out of frustration.

6.

A) Police officers who keep up to date with changing laws, policies, and community priorities tend to be more successful than those who do not, unless they are assigned to special covert details that have little contact with ordinary citizens.

B) Police officers who keep up to date with changing laws, policies, and community priorities tend to be more successful. Than those who do not unless they are assigned to special covert details that have little contact with ordinary citizens.

7.

A) Jake and Ronald were playing cards when Ronald shot Jake. In the leg.

B) Jake and Ronald were playing cards when Ronald shot Jake in the leg.

8.

A) Community leaders and law enforcement officers often work together toward common goals. Proactive problem solving and preventing social discord are two such goals.

B) Community leaders and law enforcement officers often work together toward common goals proactive problem solving and preventing social discord are two such goals.

9.

A) Detective Sherman almost got convictions for every felony arrest he ever made.

B) Detective Sherman got convictions for almost every arrest he ever made.

10.

A) Family law courtrooms are among the most dangerous because emotions run high when dealing with family issues.

B) Family law courtrooms are among the most dangerous because emotions run high. When dealing with family issues.

11.

A) Kyle wanted to sing, dance, and act; it is what made him happy.

B) Kyle wanted to sing, dance, and act; participating in the arts is what made him happy.

12.

A) Peaceful protests are part of the fabric of America. Protests are only illegal when they become unlawful assemblies or riots.

B) Peaceful protests are part of the fabric of America protests are only illegal when they become unlawful assemblies or riots.

13.

A) While happily at work downtown, Marta's house was burglarized.

B) While Marta was happily at work downtown, her house was burglarized.

14.

A) Officers collected fingerprints on print cards.

B) Fingerprints were collected by officers on print cards.

15.

A) Fran was very afraid, but she kept her fear hidden.

B) Fran was very afraid, but she kept it hidden.

VOCABULARY

Choose a word from the answer choices that is CLOSEST in meaning to the underlined word (questions 16 – 22).

16. Omari felt <u>APATHETIC</u> in his employment, so he decided to quit his job and go to law school.

    A) motivated

    B) dissatisfied

    C) indifferent

    D) unsure

17. Hank was drunk and <u>BELLIGERENT</u> because his wife left him.

    A) hostile

    B) sad

    C) angry

    D) loud

18. After years of daily observing people in the worst situations of their lives, Austin's behavior became CALLOUS.

    A) mean

    B) insensitive

    C) annoyed

    D) empathetic

19. Cheryl was nervous, but she did not want to HINDER her daughter's dream of becoming a police officer.

    A) encourage

    B) expedite

    C) crush

    D) impede

20. Clyde was LUCID when he told the paramedics who shot him.

    A) confused

    B) rational

    C) emotional

    D) incomprehensible

21. Larry thought his neighbor, John, was PILFERING Larry's morning newspaper, so he reported him to the constable.

    A) stealing

    B) borrowing

    C) moving

    D) returning

22. Blanca had an INCONSPICUOUS scar on her arm from a car accident several years earlier.

    A) large

    B) prominent

    C) unnoticeable

    D) small

Choose a word from the answer choices that is most OPPOSITE the underlined word (questions 23 – 25).

23. After working several twelve-hour shifts in a row, Deputy Nguyen developed a PERSISTENT cough.

    A) lasting

    B) intermittent

    C) unrelenting

    D) harsh

24. Case law sometimes SUPERSEDES legislated law and statutes.

    A) supports

    B) overrides

    C) submits

    D) boosts

25. If used successfully, the "heat of passion" defense can MITIGATE murder to manslaughter.

    A) lessen

    B) bolster

    C) extend

    D) change

Questions 26 – 28 provide two word choices to complete the sentences below. Choose the word that makes the most sense based on the context of the sentence.

26. The tactical commander outlined the _____ of action for the SWAT team.

    A) coarse

    B) course

27. The nightly news reported that the police apprehended the _____ killer who had been tormenting River City residents.

    A) cereal

    B) serial

28. Increased penalties for criminal activity in River City did not appear to have an _____ on the occurrence of crime.

    A) effect

    B) affect

29. Deputy Wilson worked very hard to <u>HONE</u> her skills as an officer.

  A) build

  B) sharpen

  C) steady

  D) improve

SPELLING

Read the following sentences and choose the correct spelling of the missing word (questions 31-45).

31. The jury foreman turned _____ the defendant when he read the verdict.

  A) tward

  B) toword

  C) toward

  D) tword

32. The District Attorney _____ dropped off the case files this morning.

  A) leason

  B) liason

  C) laison

  D) liaison

33. The legislature _____ the law when it was ruled unconstitutional.

  A) resinded

  B) recinded

  C) rescinded

  D) resended

34. Even the defendant was _____ when the jury returned a not guilty verdict.

  A) surprised

  B) suprised

  C) supprised

  D) surprized

30. Each year, many laws and statutes are <u>REPEALED</u>.

  A) revoked

  B) updated

  C) added

  D) reworded

35. Officer Jones had a _____ to speak loudly, which often upset people.

  A) tendancy

  B) tendency

  C) tendencie

  D) tendincy

36. Officer uses of force are _____ and appropriate actions when suspects fail to comply and can escalate police contacts in a manner that jeopardizes safety.

  A) necessary

  B) nesisarry

  C) necassery

  D) necissary

37. John Smith told the court he did not recognize the authority of the _____ and was filing a lawsuit against it to reclaim money owed him as a right of birth.

  A) goverment

  B) govermant

  C) govirnment

  D) government

38. Sasha filed a restraining order against her ex-boyfriend because he was _____ her at work.

  A) harassing

  B) harrassing

  C) harasing

  D) herassing

39. Pursuant to federal and state laws, all jails and prisons make reasonable _____ for inmates who have disabilities to ensure they have the same or comparable access as inmates who do not have disabilities.

A) acomodations

B) accommodations

C) accommadations

D) accomodations

40. Bystanders were _____ upset after witnessing such a horrific accident.

A) noticably

B) noticibly

C) noticeably

D) noticeabally

41. Jason was arrested because he was in _____ of stolen property.

A) posession

B) possesion

C) possetion

D) possession

42. River City Police Department found itself under _____ after an officer, who was chasing a dangerous criminal, crashed his patrol car into a storefront during business hours.

A) siege

B) seige

C) seege

D) seage

43. At his sentencing, Jim _____ apologized for his role in the home invasion robbery.

A) publicly

B) publicallie

C) publicaly

D) publicely

44. People who are under the influence of certain drugs can become stronger, more unpredictable, and more _____ than an average person.

A) agresive

B) aggresive

C) aggressive

D) agressive

45. Andrea worked long hours as a court reporter and often suffered headaches from extended exposure to _____ lighting.

A) floresent

B) florescint

C) flourescent

D) fluorescent

READING COMPREHENSION

The reading comprehension test measures ability to read and understand various written materials. Read each paragraph or passage and choose the response that best answers the question. All questions are self-contained and use only information provided in the passage that precedes them.

PASSAGE ONE

(1)

When people think critically, they examine, evaluate, and synthesize information they have gathered in order to arrive at a logical conclusion. Critical thinking can be accomplished at a simple or more probing level, depending on whether a cursory or more thoughtful conclusion is desired. At its most basic level, critical thinking is an activity necessary for people to function properly in society. Every day, without thought, most people engage in simple critical thinking exercises as they interact with one another. They observe, analyze, and assess clues and information around them in order to understand others' behavior and to make decisions about how to respond appropriately. When used purposefully, critical thinking can help one gain a much greater understanding of the gathered information. However, many people do not wish to move beyond this basic, instinctual level when deep critical thinking is not **imperative**. They do not wish to gain deeper understanding of a person or issue even though gaining such understanding may be as simple as asking, "Why?"

(2)

Intensive critical thinking is employed most often in academic settings. Teachers challenge students to apply a higher order of thinking skills to avoid oversimplification, to be objective, and to always ask the next question such as "Why?", "What?", or "What if?" to make reasoned judgments. Critical thinking in academia generally requires a supposition, facts and information, and the ability to infer a logical conclusion from one or more assertions. In academia, critical thinking can either be relegated to mere theoretical dialogue or be applied to an actual problem in order to generate improved conditions.

(3)

Since the 1970s, critical thinking has also been used in police work. It is vital, purposeful, and systematic. Police must analyze crimes and criminal activity, establish facts, and determine what information remains unknown. Police investigators analyze patterns and evidence to determine how and why criminal activity was committed and who committed the crime. They ask the questions "What's missing?", "What are the benefits of the crime?", "Who benefited?", "Was the crime planned or opportunistic?" Each question probes deeper into the issue and helps investigators uncover clues to reconstruct other people's reasoning. Critical thinking in police work questions the known facts of a case in such a way that investigators are able to understand criminal actions, and those who commit them, more accurately. Such thinking can help investigators understand a perpetrator's state of mind, determine what the perpetrator was thinking, how he or she was thinking, as well as establish the investigator's opinion of what, how, and why a particular event occurred.

(4)

Recently, critical thinking has become even more vital to law enforcement because criminals continue to become more **savvy**. As technology has evolved, so has crime sophistication. Criminals have to work smarter to avoid being apprehended, thus detectives work smarter by studying, evaluating, and assessing evidence to successfully investigate and prosecute criminals.

46. The tone of the author can be best described as:

    A) objective

    B) argumentative

    C) passionate

    D) empathetic

47. As used in paragraph 1, what is the best synonym for *imperative*:

    A) absolutely necessary

    B) very important

    C) of personal interest

    D) avoidable

48. According to the passage, it can be inferred that the author believes which of the following:

    I. Critical thinking is used in many ways.

    II. Critical thinking is only important in academia.

    III. Critical thinking is vital in police work.

    A) III only

    B) II only

    C) II and III only

    D) I and III only

49. As used in paragraph 4, what is the best definition of *savvy*?

    A) cool

    B) shrewd

    C) inexperienced

    D) dangerous

50. Which of the following, if true, WEAKENS the main point of paragraph 3?

    A) People do not use critical thinking in everyday life.

    B) Law enforcement began using critical thinking methods in the 1990s.

    C) Academics do not apply theory to real-life situations.

    D) Critical thinking has reduced successful investigations and prosecutions of crimes.

51. What is the best title for this passage?

    A) The Definition of Critical Thinking

    B) Critical Thinking and Law Enforcement

    C) The Many Applications of Critical Thinking

    D) Critical Thinking: A Survey

52. According to the passage, what is the main reason for the application of critical thinking in police work?

    A) to help investigators understand criminal activity and criminal perpetrators more accurately

    B) to determine how criminal activity was committed and who committed the crime

    C) because crime sophistication has evolved, and thus investigators must also evolve

    D) all of the above

Passage Two

River City Police Department policy mandates that officers remain in good physical condition while employed with the department. Most officers would gladly comply, but commute times, long work hours, and mandatory overtime account for about fifteen hours of each officer's day. Officers recently asked River City about developing a wellness program for staff members, sworn staff in particular, including the ability to exercise in one of the many gyms located at various River City Police Department's satellite facilities. The resulting memo from the River City chief of police was disseminated to all staff.

Dear Staff,

It gives me great pleasure to work at an agency that is full of hardworking, motivated individuals, sworn and civilians alike, who seek new ways to continue improving themselves in both professional and personal life.

As you are aware, law enforcement is a physical job that requires the men and women who do the job to maintain a high level of physical fitness. I'm confident all of you would like to maintain that high level of physical fitness. I know this is difficult for many who have family obligations and long commutes from your respective homes in the outlying areas, and for those who work copious overtime shifts. These factors have undoubtedly created barriers for you to reach your personal goals and the required baseline goals of this department.

It was recently brought to my attention that a number of you requested permission to exercise at your duty station during your workday, on your meal break, in one of the various gyms we maintain on facility sites, in order to make exercising easier to fit into your daily routine. I understand your various dilemmas, but for reasons of liability, workers' compensation issues, as well as the logistical issues involved in managing meal breaks so an entire duty station is not working out at the same time, I must deny that request. I will, however, work with you in other ways to help you meet your fitness goals.

As of next week, the following policies will take effect under the River City Police Employee Wellness Pledge program:

- We will update our meal program for staff members assigned to duty stations where leaving base during shifts is disallowed. We will no longer provide hamburgers, soda, french fries, bacon, or chips. For those of you who work the night shift and eat breakfast, eggs and hash brown potatoes will still be available. If you would like to purchase a soda or snack during your twelve-hour shift, you may do so at the remaining vending machines on-site.
- You may not exercise at any gym during duty hours, even if you are on break. You are welcome to work out before or after your assigned shift at any of our gyms.
- We will begin a physical fitness club that will meet once a month at one of our facilities for organized workouts. This club is open to the first 30 people who sign up. I, as well as the **warriors** who already work out with me, would love for you to join us at our morning gym sessions.

Thank you for your diligence to do the job well and to make River City the best police department in the state. I look forward to helping you meet your fitness goals and to your feedback on this exciting new program.

Keep up the good work!

Sincerely,

Chief Jeff Hyde

53. What is the main point of the chief's letter?

A) Physical fitness is important for police work.

B) The chief is willing to help officers and staff stay fit.

C) The chief does not want to be responsible for staff who exercise on duty.

D) It is primarily the responsibility of the employee to manage time for workouts.

54. According to the chief, what is the main reason he denied the request to work out during work hours?

A) Staff should be working, not exercising.

B) Even though staff may be on break, River City is still liable for injuries.

C) It is difficult logistically to ensure not all staff are working out at the same time.

D) Both B and C are correct.

55. What is the overall tone of the chief's letter?

A) cordial

B) angry

C) passionate

D) overbearing

56. What is the best meaning of the word *warriors* as used in the passage?

A) a person experienced in warfare

B) a person who shows great vigor

C) a person skilled in using weapons

D) a person with fitness experience

57. According to the passage, how many hours in a given day does the average River City officer have left to eat, sleep, run errands, and work out after working the assigned shift?

A) fifteen

B) seventeen

C) nine

D) eleven

PASSAGE THREE

These days, it is harder than ever for kids to simply "walk away" from a bully. Bullying among children and adolescents has evolved beyond taunting a smaller or less popular kid while he or she is at school, to cyber stalking children across city and state lines with the use of common electronic devices. Because of the increasing reach of bullies, among other things, suicides and violent confrontations among youth have risen over the years.

Because of the current scope of bullying, school administrators no longer rely solely on teachers to keep kids safe while at school. Rather, administrators build teams of collaborators that include health care workers, teachers, administration, security staff, and law enforcement personnel to ensure schools remain a safe place for kids to learn. School resource officers (SROs) receive training in issues that are unique to youth. Generally, SROs have an office on campus. They are stationed at the school and spend their time dealing with law enforcement issues. They also spend a great deal of time talking to kids about anything that interests them, such as school activities, sports, law enforcement, and life in general. Since SROs talk to kids at particular schools regularly, officers are in a unique position to identify emerging issues and prevent them before they develop into greater problems.

SROs play a large role in managing situations that involve bullying so that *all* involved students and families are heard and respected.

58. Which fact, if true, strengthens the author's main point?

A) More kids are bullied currently than in previous years.

B) The majority of bullying happens on school grounds.

C) Funding for school resource officers has been reduced.

D) Youth suicides are on the decline.

59. According to the passage, why are SROs important for managing bullying?

A) SROs arrest students who are too aggressive.

B) SROs get to know students and can prevent problems.

C) SROs provide defensive training for victims of bullies.

D) SROs help teachers learn to identify bullies.

60. According to the passage, why has bullying become so prevalent?

   A) increased negative behavior

   B) school resource officers on school grounds

   C) technological advancement

   D) boredom among children

PASSAGE FOUR

With over twenty-two million staff members and students on college campuses across the nation, campus security has moved to the spotlight. Security staff have the opportunity to be proactive, educating the college community about campus life and being safe while in a home away from home.

Depending on the size and location of a given school, campus security staffing and scope might be either small-scale or **monolithically** entrenched in the campus community. Additionally, some campuses employ full-time police agencies, while others employ independent contractors or private security companies. However, because the nature and scope of each campus security department varies so widely, the level of communication with other security and law enforcement departments also varies, causing misunderstandings and errors in interdepartmental communication. Now is a crucial time, given the tragic events on school and college campuses and the sheer number of people continually on campuses, to begin creating universal standards so that all students and staff members have the same level of protection regardless of the school where they choose to study or work.

61. As used in the passage, what is the best definition of the word *monolithically*?

   A) stonelike

   B) impenetrable

   C) massive

   D) minuscule

62. According to the passage, what types of agencies are employed as campus security?

   A) security companies

   B) law enforcement

   C) contractors

   D) all of the above

63. According to the passage, what is an important problem that needs to be addressed?

   A) communication among agencies

   B) size of security agencies

   C) education of the campus community

   D) universal standards of protection

64. Which of the following, if true, most WEAKENS the argument that the variation in size and scope of campus security departments is the cause of communication problems?

   A) Smaller operations have more money to spend on communications than large ones.

   B) Interoperability between campuses is based on size and scope.

   C) Each operation, regardless of size and scope, uses its own dedicated communication system.

   D) Full-time police agencies have more capabilities than independent contractors.

65. Based on the tone of the passage, it can be inferred that the author believes which statement about campus security?

   A) Campus security operations are varied to the point of dysfunction.

   B) Size and scope do not necessarily matter if the operation functions properly.

   C) Large campus security operations are safer than small ones.

   D) Small campus security operations have better communications capabilities.

CLOZE

On this part of the test, fill in each blank with the appropriate word. The words are indicated by blank spaces and dashes within the passage. Each dash represents a letter. The word must be correct, given the context of the passage, and it must have the same number of letters as dashes. All words that meet both criteria are considered correct. More than one word may be appropriate for a given space.

More than twenty-five years ago, law enforcement first partnered with community leaders in an attempt to bridge the gap between the police and the communities they serve. Law enforcement had long since realized _ _ _ _ _ _ _ _ changes were making it more and _ _ _ _ difficult to do the job without _ _ _ _ _ _ _ _ support. Because police could not do _ _ _ job alone, and thus did the _ _ _ poorly in certain communities, community trust _ _ _ _ _ to falter. The creation of community _ _ _ _ _ _ _ _ programs was a way to rebuild _ _ _ community trust as well as to reinvigorate _ _ and allow police to do their _ _ _ better. Initial community policing programs were _ _ _ _ _ _ _ _ _ designed to help community members mobilize _ _ _ _ _ _ _ and resources to solve problems, voice _ _ _ _ _ concerns, contribute advice, and take action _ _ address concerns. But these initial programs tended to be paternalistic, and while some _ _ _ _ _ _ _ _ _ _ showed improvement, the improvement was slow. _ _ other communities, residents and leaders outright _ _ _ _ _ _ _ _ the efforts of the police to _ _ _ _ together.

Over the years, community policing _ _ _ _ _ _ _. This evolution reflected moving away from the paternalism of _ _ _ _ programs and toward more true collaboration. _ _ _ _ _ _ than simply "voicing opinions," which police _ _ _ _ took under advisement while determining an action _ _ _ _, community members became bona fide stakeholders _ _ _ _ equal control over community priorities and _ _ _ _ _ plans. Today, community policing exists as _ collaborative effort between police and these community _ _ _ _ _ _ _ _ _ _ _ such as schools, community-based organizations, local large and small _ _ _ _ _ _ _ _ _ _ _, local government, and residents, and is designed to _ _ _ _ _ _ _ _, prioritize, and solve community problems. Across the United States, the _ _ _ _ _ _ _ _ community policing philosophy promotes organizational strategies _ _ _ _ use this collaboration to problem-solve _ _ _ proactively address persistent or emerging public _ _ _ _ _ _ problems such as crime and social _ _ _ _ _ _ _ _. All current community programs must be _ _ _ _ _ on three essential components: _ _ _ _ _ _ _ _ _ _ _ _ partnerships; organizational transformation to support these collaborative partnerships as well as to support _ _ _ _ _ _ -solving methods; and a proactive, systemic _ _ _ _ _ _ _ _ _ _ of identified issues. This examination should also explore effective response evaluation. As a _ _ _ _ _ _, models of community policing exist in most police agencies across the nation and the communities they serve, crisis situations have decreased in many communities, and the police have a markedly improved relationship with the citizens they _ _ _ _ _.

ANSWER KEY

WRITING

CLARITY

1. **B) is correct.** Answer A is a run-on sentence.

2. **A) is correct.** Answer B contains a vague reference. It is not clear whose supervisor wishes to speak with which employee.

3. **A) is correct.** Answer B contains a sentence fragment: "As she made the right turn."

4. **B) is correct.** Answer A contains a misplaced modifier. It is not clear if officers who train are caught off guard infrequently, or if officers who train infrequently are caught off guard. Answer B is a clearer sentence.

5. **A) is correct.** Answer B is a run-on sentence.

6. **A) is correct.** Answer B contains a sentence fragment; the phrase "Than those who do not unless they are assigned to special covert details that have little contact with ordinary citizens" is not a complete sentence.

7. **B) is correct.** Answer A contains a sentence fragment ("In the leg").

8. **A) is correct.** Answer B is a run-on sentence. It requires a semicolon after *common goals*, or the sentence should be broken up into two as in answer choice A.

9. **B) is correct.** Answer A contains a misplaced modifier and is unclear. Choice A states, "Detective Sherman *almost* got convictions," which implies he got acquittals instead. Choice B is clearer, as the word *almost* modifies *every arrest*, rather than *convictions*.

10. **A) is correct.** Answer B contains a sentence fragment: "When dealing with family issues."

11. **B) is correct.** Answer choice A contains a vague reference; it is not clear whether singing, dancing, acting, or all three made Kyle happy. Choice B is clearer.

12. **A) is correct.** Answer B is a run-on sentence. The sentence should be broken up into two, as in answer choice A, or connected with a semicolon after *America*.

13. **B) is correct.** Answer choice A contains a dangling modifier. The phrase "While happily at work downtown" is modifying "Marta's house" instead of Marta. It appears as if "Marta's house" is "happily at work."

14. **A) is correct.** Answer choice B contains a misplaced modifier. It is not clear whether the officers or the fingerprints are on the print cards. Choice A is written more clearly, with *Officers* as the subject and using the active verb *collected*.

15. **A) is correct.** Answer choice B contains a vague reference, using the pronoun *it*. It is not clear what Fran kept hidden. Answer choice A is more clearly written, specifying what Fran kept hidden: "her fear."

VOCABULARY

16. **C) is correct.** *Apathetic* means *indifferent*. Omari might also be unsatisfied with his work, but *dissatisfied* is not the best answer here. He is the opposite of *motivated*. If he were *unsure* about his work, he might not be so quick to leave it.

17. **A) is correct.** *Belligerent* means *hostile*. The other answer choices—*sad*, *angry*, and *loud*—are not the best answers because a person may exhibit any of those characteristics without being hostile or combative.

18. **B) is correct.** *Callous* means *insensitive*. A person may be *mean* or *annoyed* without being insensitive, so answer choices A and C are not the best choices. Answer choice D— *empathetic*—means the opposite of *callous* or *insensitive*.

19. **D) is correct.** To *hinder* means to *impede*. To *impede* is less severe than to *crush*, which is to destroy something. Both *encourage* and *expedite* imply helping something to happen, which is the opposite meaning.

20. **B) is correct.** *Lucid* means *rational* or *clear*. Answer choices A and D—*confused* and *incomprehensible*—are the opposite of *rational*. Clyde may have been *emotional*, but that does not explain why he was able to describe a person while in a stressful situation.

21. **A) is correct.** *Pilfering* means *stealing*. If John had been *borrowing*, *moving*, or *returning* the newspaper, it is unlikely that Larry would have taken such drastic action.

22. **C) is correct.** *Inconspicuous* means *unnoticeable*. Answer choice B, *prominent*, means the opposite. Answer choices A and D—*large* and *small*—are not the best choices because

both large and small items could be inconspicuous.

23. **B) is correct.** *Intermittent* is the opposite of *persistent*. Answers A and C, *lasting* and *unrelenting*, are synonyms. *Harsh* is unconnected because both an intermittent and a persistent cough could be harsh.

24. **C) is correct.** *Submits* is the opposite of *supersede*. *Overrides* is a synonym for *supersedes*. *Supports* and *boosts* are closer in meaning to *supersedes*, though not exactly the same, as they fail to imply the sense of overruling; in any case, they are not opposite in meaning to *supersedes*.

25. **B) is correct.** *Bolster* is the opposite of *mitigate*. Answer A, *lessen*, is a synonym. The other choices, *extend* and *change*, do not relate to *mitigate*.

26. **B) is correct.** In this context, *course* means "manner of procedure." *Coarse* is a homonym and means "harsh" or "grating."

27. **B) is correct.** In this context, *serial* means "producing a series of similar actions," such as killing. *Cereal* is an edible grain.

28. **A) is correct.** *Effect* as used in this context is a noun. Generally (though there are exceptions), the word *affect* is a verb, and *effect* is a noun. To *affect* is to "act upon something to cause change," as in "The snow *affected* his ability to drive." An *effect* is a result, as in "The snow had a negative *effect* on the undercarriage of his car." In the exam question, the "increased penalties" had no *effect* on crime.

29. **B) is correct.** To *hone* is to *sharpen*. *Build* and *improve* are close in meaning to *hone* but are not synonyms. *Steady* is unrelated.

30. A) is correct. *Repealed* means *revoked*. *Updated*, *added*, and *reworded* would imply the opposite.

31. C) is correct. Choice C, *toward*, is spelled right.

32. D) is correct. Choice D, *liaison*, is spelled right.

33. C) is correct. Choice C, *rescinded*, is spelled right.

34. A) is correct. Choice A, *surprised*, is spelled right.

35. B) is correct. Choice B, *tendency*, is spelled right.

36. A) is correct. Choice A, *necessary*, is spelled right.

37. D) is correct. Choice D, *government*, is spelled right.

38. A) is correct. Choice A, *harassing*, is spelled right.

39. B) is correct. Choice B, *accommodations*, is spelled right.

40. C) is correct. Choice C, *noticeably*, is spelled right.

41. D) is correct. Choice D, *possession*, is spelled right.

42. A) is correct. Choice A, *siege*, is spelled right.

43. A) is correct. Choice A, *publicly*, is spelled right.

44. C) is correct. Choice C, *aggressive*, is spelled right.

45. D) is correct. Choice D, *fluorescent*, is spelled right.

READING COMPREHENSION

46. A) is correct. The passage is written with an impersonal objective tone, much like an article or news report, rather than to persuade or debate. It is not argumentative, passionate, or empathetic.

47. A) is correct. In this context, *imperative* means "absolutely necessary." The passage asserts that "many people do not wish to move beyond this basic, instinctual level" of thought to critical thinking unless they must. It must be essential for them to engage in critical thinking, not just important or interesting (choices B and C). Choice D, *avoidable*, is not relevant here.

48. D) is correct. Only I and III are true. Option II, which states critical thinking is *only* important in academia, contradicts the first sentence of paragraph 3: "Since the 1970s, critical thinking has also been used in police work." In fact, the point of the passage is that critical thinking is vital to police work (choice III).

49. B) is correct. The definition of *savvy* is *shrewd*. This paragraph states that policing requires critical thinking to outsmart criminals. Choice A, *cool*, is not relevant here. *Inexperienced* is the opposite meaning; a savvy criminal would likely be quite experienced. And *dangerous* criminals are not necessarily savvy.

50. D) is correct. If fewer crimes were successfully investigated and prosecuted since police began using critical thinking in investigations, then it would appear critical thinking is not helpful in police work. The purpose of paragraph 3 is to illustrate the many ways critical thinking has been used and can help in law enforcement. Answers A, B, and C are incorrect because they misstate facts or ideas from the passage.

51. B) is correct. The best title for this passage is "Critical Thinking and Law Enforcement." Although the passage defines critical thinking and illustrates its various applications, the bulk of the passage talks about the application of critical thinking to law enforcement. Thus answer B is the best choice.

52. **D) is correct.** Each point was presented as an important reason critical thinking is used in law enforcement.

53. **D) is correct.** The chief's letter identifies personal reasons why many people cannot schedule exercise into their daily routines. It also mentions the "warriors" who do work out in the morning, and the liability issues around allowing staff to exercise during shifts. Thus, D is the best answer; the chief will help, but he puts the responsibility on the employee to manage his or her time.

54. **D) is correct.** The chief notes both logistics and liability as reasons why he denied the request.

55. **A) is correct.** The tone of the letter is cordial. The letter uses mostly friendly and supportive words in a professional format. The chief begins his letter by applauding employees for wanting to meet standards. He clearly explains the reasoning for his own choices in changing policy by taking away food options and prohibiting exercise on meal breaks. While it is debatable whether those choices are good policy for the officers, the tone of the letter is not angry or overbearing, ruling out choices B and D. He does express enthusiasm for the "warriors" he already works out with and says they would "love" other officers to join them, but this is more enthusiastic than overbearing, ruling out choice C.

56. **B) is correct.** As used in the passage, the chief implies the "warriors" who work out every morning with him show motivation, energy, and a willingness to do what it takes to fit exercise into their schedules. Warfare and weapons are irrelevant to this passage. Finally, the chief does not suggest that those who work out with him are exceptionally experienced; otherwise, he would not invite those officers looking to improve their fitness to join them.

57. **C) is correct.** The introduction to the passage states that most officers spend fifteen hours a day working and commuting. There are twenty-four hours in a day; fifteen subtracted from twenty-four leaves nine hours remaining.

58. **A) is correct.** The author's main point is that bullying has increased in scope from years past. If the number of children being bullied has increased, this strengthens the author's argument. The author asserts that bullying occurs beyond school, thanks to technology, making answer choice B incorrect. The passage discusses SROs at length, so if there were less funding for SROs, the argument would be weakened, making C incorrect. Finally, the passage states that youth suicides are increasing, so choice D directly contradicts the passage, making it incorrect.

59. **B) is correct.** According to the passage, "SROs talk to kids at particular schools regularly," so "officers are in a unique position to identify emerging issues and prevent them before they develop into greater problems." The passage never states that SROs arrest bullies, just that SROs "are stationed at the school and spend their time dealing with law enforcement issues." SROs do not offer training; they "receive training in issues that are unique to youth." The passage never states specifically that SROs show teachers how to identify bullies, just that all personnel work together "to ensure schools remain a safe place for kids to learn."

60. **C) is correct.** The passage immediately asserts that technological advancement has made bullying more prevalent. The first paragraph states that "[b]ullying among children and adolescents has evolved…to cyber stalking children across city and state lines with the use of common electronic devices." The passage explains that school resource officers enhance safety at school, so B is not correct. Finally, the passage never mentions more negative behavior among children or boredom as factors in bullying, ruling out answer choices A and D.

61. **C) is correct.** *Monolithically* means *massively*. It can also mean *stonelike*, but in this context choice C is the better answer; the passage suggests the agency is massive in contrast to "small-scale." This comparison makes choice

C better than choice B, *impenetrable. Minuscule*, choice D, means the opposite.

62. D) is correct. The passage mentions security companies, law enforcement, and contractors as agencies employed as campus security.

63. A) is correct. According to the passage, "[b]ecause the nature and scope of each campus security department varies so widely, the level of communication with other security and law enforcement departments also varies, causing misunderstandings and errors in interdepartmental communication." The passage mentions the type and size of various security agencies as a reason communication is a problem, but the overarching problem is communication, so choice A is a better answer than choice B. The passage states that "educating the college community about campus life and being safe while in a home away from home" is the job of campus security, not a problem, making choice C incorrect. Finally, the author suggests "to begin creating universal standards" for protection. Universal standards are not a problem but are a possible solution to problems.

64. C) is correct. The passage mentions that the varying size and scope of different agencies make it difficult for them to communicate with one another. If each agency used its own dedicated communication system, then these communication systems would be the reason for interagency communication problems rather than the variation in size and scope of the agencies. Choices A, B, and D support the author's argument, because they assert that the ability of an agency to communicate effectively is based on its size.

65. B) is correct. The author does not make a judgment about any specific type of security agency. Therefore, it can be inferred from the passage that the author believes that size and scope of a security department or operation do not matter as long as the operation functions properly.

CLOZE

More than twenty-five years ago, law enforcement first partnered with community leaders in an attempt to bridge the gap between the police and the communities they serve. Law enforcement had long since realized **S O C I E T A L** changes were making it more and **M O R E** difficult to do the job without **C O M M U N I T Y** support. Because police could not do **T H E** job alone, and thus did the **J O B** poorly in certain communities, community trust **B E G A N** to falter. The creation of community **P O L I C I N G** programs was a way to rebuild **T H E** community trust as well as to reinvigorate **I T** and allow police to do their **J O B** better. Initial community policing programs were **P R I M A R I L Y** designed to help community members mobilize **S U P P O R T** and resources to solve problems, voice **T H E I R** concerns, contribute advice, and take action **T O** address concerns. But these initial programs tended to be paternalistic, and while some **C O M M U N I T I E S** showed improvement, the improvement was slow. **I N** other communities, residents and leaders outright **R E S I S T E D** the efforts of the police to **W O R K** together.

Over the years, community policing **E V O L V E D**. This evolution reflected moving away from the paternalism of **O L D** programs and toward more true collaboration. **R A T H E R** than simply "voicing opinions," which police **T H E N** took under advisement while determining an action **P L A N**, community members became bona fide stakeholders **W I T H** equal control over community priorities and **A C T I O N** plans. Today, community policing exists as **A** collaborative effort between police and these community **S T A K E H O L D E R S** such as schools, community-based organizations, local large and small **B U S I N E S S E S**, local government, and residents, and is designed to **I D E N T I F Y**, prioritize, and solve community problems. Across the United States, the **N A T I O N A L** community policing philosophy promotes organizational strategies **T H A T** use this collaboration to problem-solve **A N D** proactively address persistent or emerging public **S A F E T Y** problems such as crime and social **D I S O R D E R**. All current community programs must be **B A S E D** on three essential components: **C O L L A B O R A T I V E** partnerships; organizational transformation to support these collaborative partnerships as well as to support **P R O B L E M**-solving methods; and a proactive, systemic **E X A M I N A T I O N** of identified issues. This examination should also explore effective response evaluation. As a **R E S U L T**, models of community policing exist in most police agencies across the nation and the communities they serve, crisis situations have decreased in many communities, and the police have a markedly improved relationship with the citizens they **S E R V E**.

PRACTICE TEST TWO

WRITING

The writing test measures three aspects of good writing: clarity, vocabulary, and spelling.

CLARITY

In the following sentence pairs, identify the sentence that is most clearly written.

1.

A) The bus driver lost control of the bus while turning a corner. Too fast.

B) The bus driver lost control of the bus while turning a corner too fast.

2.

A) Steven saw his stolen car on the way to work.

B) On the way to work, Steven saw his stolen car.

3.

A) Jared drank several alcoholic beverages at the party. He crashed into a parked car on the way home and was arrested for DUI.

B) Jared drank several alcoholic beverages at the party he crashed into a parked car on the way home and was arrested for DUI.

4.

A) Officer Daryn said he did not like to drive in pursuits because the fast speeds make you sick.

B) Officer Daryn said he did not like to drive in pursuits because the fast speeds make him sick.

5.

A) Generally, most people remain unaware of the judicial system's process. Unless they become a party to an action.

B) Generally, most people remain unaware of the judicial system's process unless they become a party to an action.

6.

A) As the defendant was remanded into custody, the judge lectured him.

B) The judge lectured the defendant as he was remanded into custody.

7.

A) Court clerks are essential members of the court staff they maintain all the court documents and record each word spoken in court while "on the record."

B) Court clerks are essential members of the court staff. They maintain all the court documents and record each word spoken in court while "on the record."

8.

A) Jack called the Sheriff's Office, but they did not return his call.

B) Jack called the Sheriff's Office, but the answering service did not return his call.

9.

A) Greg's neighbor has a dog. That barks all hours of the day and night.

B) Greg's neighbor has a dog that barks all hours of the day and night.

10.

A) Officer Martinez reported the stolen car.

B) The car was reported stolen by Officer Martinez.

11.

A) Community policing is not a new concept it has, however, recently received a face-lift.

B) Community policing is not a new concept. It has, however, recently received a face-lift.

12.

A) Eagerly awaiting time off, Ebony's vacation was just about to start.

B) Eagerly awaiting time off, Ebony was just about to start her vacation.

13.

A) Stoplights are often timed for safety when drivers "jump" the green, they are cheating the system, and the results could be deadly.

B) Stoplights are often timed for safety. When drivers "jump" the green, they are cheating the system, and the results could be deadly.

14.

A) Inmates received lunches in bags from deputies.

B) Inmates received lunches from deputies in bags.

15.

A) Every time Alonzo turned on the TV, they said another city was experiencing unrest.

B) Every time Alonzo turned on the TV, the news reported another city was experiencing unrest.

VOCABULARY

Choose a word from the answer choices that is CLOSEST in meaning to the underlined word (questions 16 – 22).

16. Julian became <u>FRANTIC</u> when he realized his child was missing.

    A) frenzied

    B) calm

    C) frustrated

    D) upset

17. Henry only <u>EXACERBATED</u> the problem when he poured water on a grease fire.

    A) hurt

    B) reduced

    C) aggravated

    D) excited

18. Deputy Hanes writes reports that tend to be <u>VERBOSE</u>.

    A) concise

    B) clear

    C) confusing

    D) wordy

19. One purpose of community policing is to <u>FOSTER</u> relationships between the police and the communities they serve.

    A) alleviate

    B) create

    C) discourage

    D) promote

20. It is impossible to QUANTIFY the damage resulting from the fire.

  A) measure

  B) understand

  C) extend

  D) improve

21. The jury came to a DUBIOUS conclusion based on the evidence.

  A) dishonest

  B) questionable

  C) obvious

  D) definite

22. Officers FURTIVELY infiltrated the gang in order to gather intelligence.

  A) stealthily

  B) fraudulently

  C) brazenly

  D) openly

Choose a word from the answer choices that is most OPPOSITE the underlined word (questions 23 – 25).

23. Judge Singleton ABDICATED her seat on the bench because she was seriously ill.

  A) left

  B) maintained

  C) abandoned

  D) relinquished

24. The jury was admonished and advised that they could not DEVIATE from the instructions.

  A) diverge

  B) depart

  C) sway

  D) remain

25. Toby made his way to the top with GUILE and swindled thousands of people out of millions of dollars.

  A) duplicity

  B) assistance

  C) honesty

  D) savvy

Questions 26 – 28 provide two word choices to complete the sentences below. Choose the word that makes the most sense based on the context of the sentence.

26. When Tom spoke at the town hall meeting, he intended his words to motivate people to fight for their rights, not to _____ a riot.

  A) incite

  B) insight

27. Mayor Brighton did not _____ whether Oscar's speech was protected by the First Amendment of the Constitution.

  A) know

  B) no

28. Jerry had not eaten in four days and had no money, so he decided to _____ some food to get by.

  A) steel

  B) steal

Choose the best synonym for the underlined word from the answer choices below (questions 29 – 30).

29. Some criminals manage to have an AFFABLE demeanor despite the atrocity of their crimes.

  A) warm

  B) friendly

  C) angry

  D) wonderful

30. Sally <u>ALIENATED</u> all her family and friends when she became addicted to drugs.

  A) angered

  B) estranged

  C) frustrated

  D) united

SPELLING

Read the following sentences and choose the correct spelling of the missing word.

31. The relationship of the prosecution and the defense is _____ by design.

  A) adversarial

  B) advirsarial

  C) advirsareal

  D) adverserial

32. The judge ruled the information was not _____ to the case and was thus inadmissible.

  A) germain

  B) germean

  C) girmain

  D) germane

33. The tension in the courtroom was _____ as the jury prepared to read the verdict.

  A) palpible

  B) palpable

  C) palpebal

  D) palpabal

34. The judge signed a _____ to compel the company to turn the phone records over to the police.

  A) supena

  B) suppena

  C) subpoena

  D) supeana

35. Judy was _____ of her son, who suddenly had a lot of money and rarely came home at night.

  A) suspisious

  B) suspisios

  C) suspiscious

  D) suspicious

36. At the scene of a car accident, Officer Garcia attempted to _____ the exchange of information between drivers because they were arguing with each other.

  A) fasilitate

  B) fascilitate

  C) facilitate

  D) facilatate

37. The suspect was _____ for four hours before he confessed.

  A) interrogated

  B) interogated

  C) interragated

  D) interagated

38. Four _____ witnesses placed Harry at the scene of the crime.

  A) indapendant

  B) independent

  C) independant

  D) indapendent

39. As a victim of a _____ crime, Luis devoted his time to changing legislation regarding victims' rights.

    A) heinous

    B) hanous

    C) haneous

    D) hienous

40. Gabriel was an _____ child who would not listen to his parents and continued to get into trouble.

    A) incorrigable

    B) inccorigable

    C) incorrigeable

    D) incorrigible

41. Officer Sasser knew the importance of attention to detail and never performed her duties in a _____ manner.

    A) perfunctary

    B) perfunctory

    C) perfunctiry

    D) perfunctery

42. Sovereign citizens are people who belong to a _____ organization and refuse to recognize the authority of the United States.

    A) seditious

    B) seditiuos

    C) saditious

    D) siditious

43. The president of the neighborhood watch called the police and requested a house be placed under _____ because its occupants were suspected of drug dealing.

    A) survailance

    B) surveillance

    C) survielance

    D) servielance

42. Stella survived her attack because she was _____.

    A) tenacious

    B) tinasious

    C) tenasious

    D) tanancious

44. Ed was arrested for _____ because he was drunk and sleeping on a park bench at two o'clock in the afternoon.

    A) vagrency

    B) vagrincie

    C) vagrincy

    D) vagrancy

READING COMPREHENSION

The reading comprehension test measures ability to read and understand various written materials. Read each paragraph or passage and choose the response that best answers the question. All questions are self-contained and use only information provided in the passage that precedes them.

PASSAGE ONE

(1)

Since the police usually do not have the opportunity to watch a crime as it happens, they must rely on evidence, statements from witnesses and involved parties, and deduction skills to draw conclusions about what actually occurred. Although reliance on information from others is essential, the information officers receive is often inaccurate either because the individual was mistaken in his or her perception, was biased, or was purposefully deceptive. Police must skillfully sift through all the information they receive and decide which is accurate and which is not. The officer's decision is generally based on his or her assessment of the information's source and whether it is credible or reliable. There are three main reasons information is unreliable.

(2)

The most frequent type of unreliable information is mistaken perception. Mistaken perception happens when otherwise honest and reliable people give information they believe to be true but is not. Mistaken perception can happen for a number of reasons. For example, during a stressful situation the brain releases adrenaline into the body, causing physiological changes. During periods of extreme stress, blood rushes away from nonessential organs and systems toward the heart. As this happens, people often experience various sensory disturbances, like time anomalies. Often witnesses and involved parties will report that a greater or lesser amount of time passed than actually did. A time **anomaly** affects an individual's sense of time, which appears to be moving at lightning speed or in slow motion. Sight and sound may also be affected. Witnesses and involved parties experiencing auditory occlusion often describe a temporary loss or lessening of hearing; sounds are muted or unheard. People also experience the feeling of tunnel vision, wherein peripheral vision is diminished and they can only see what is directly in front of them. People who undergo these physiological changes, even when mild, may have a distorted perception of the incident even though they are telling the truth based on their recollection. Police officers must pay attention to behavior cues that signal an individual may have altered perception due to physiological disturbances.

(3)

Another issue with involved party reliability is individual bias. While some people have biases they are aware of, sometimes people have biases they are unaware of for a number of reasons. The bias may stem from accepting another source of information as true without question. In other words, the individual was uncritical of the information received and then passed along to police. People also may have a bias due to a vested interest in a particular view or outcome, and their perception is altered by that interest. Police officers must be diligent in identifying any possible biases during the interview process when establishing witness accuracy and reliability.

(4)

Lastly, there are times when people are simply dishonest. The reason for their dishonesty may have nothing to do with the situation at hand. The motivation for the dishonesty may or may not be relevant to the incident, but it is crucial when determining the reliability of the statement itself. If a person is willing to be dishonest to the police, for whatever reason, his or her credibility must also be called into question. Police officers must pay attention to accounts of an incident by witnesses and involved parties for inconsistencies and **blatant** misinformation.

(5)

There are many reasons why accounts of an incident by witnesses and involved parties might be unreliable. It is the officer's duty to use critical thinking, deduction, and logical reasoning to determine what is or is not reliable and why. Police officers have a variety of tools at their disposal in order to determine the accuracy of witness or involved party statements. Corroboration, witness expertise, police officer observations, evidence located at the scene, and the like, can help an officer analyze the information to determine the probable reliability of a statement.

46. What is the main point of this article?

   A) Witnesses are dishonest.

   B) Witnesses can be unreliable.

   C) Stress can alter witnesses' perception.

   D) Biased witnesses are unreliable.

47. The passage implies which of the following?

   A) Because witnesses are often unreliable, officers must be diligent in their investigation.

   B) Witnesses are never reliable; officers must use other evidence to prove crimes.

   C) The most frequent type of unreliable information is individual bias.

   D) Only some witnesses should be trusted, but it is impossible to tell who is reliable.

48. According to this article, what is the main reason for problems with witness reliability?

   A) dishonesty

   B) mistaken perception

   C) bias

   D) all of the above

49. According to the passage, which of the following is true?

   A) People only lie for reasons related to the situation.

   B) Some people are unaware of bias they hold.

   C) During high-stress situations, blood rushes away from the heart.

   D) Witnesses' perception of time is generally quite accurate.

50. According to the passage, what is auditory occlusion?

   A) total loss of hearing

   B) tunnel vision

   C) a temporary loss or lessening of hearing

   D) a sensory disturbance

51. What is the best synonym for the word *anomaly* as it is used in paragraph 2 of the passage?

   A) commonality

   B) ambivalence

   C) abnormality

   D) uncertainty

52. What word below is the best meaning of the word *blatant* as it is used in paragraph 4 of the passage?

   A) obvious

   B) flagrant

   C) subtle

   D) implied

Passage Two

(1)

Think cattle rustling is a thing of the past? Think again. As of March 2014, cattle rustling in the western United States is still "a thing." Ranchers and law enforcement are **diligently** working together to protect herds and keep them safe from a brand-new threat—meth addicts. People addicted to methamphetamine have turned in their climbing boots and copper wire–grabbing gloves to steal cows in order to finance their drug habits. Where's the *Outlaw Josey Wales* when you need him?

(2)

Levity aside, neither of the aforementioned issues is a laughing matter. Methamphetamine addiction is very serious, dangerous, and expensive to maintain. Issues surrounding the crime of cow theft is equally serious, dangerous, and expensive. Cows are valuable and can be sold at auction for around $1,000 a head. A local news station obtained video depicting thieves as they stole an entire pen of cows by coaxing them into the back of a big rig in the middle of the night. Another rancher had 100 cows stolen. At $1,000 a head, that's big money—and big jail time. Currently, cattle rustling carries penalties of up to ten years in prison. The problem for ranchers, while fortuitous for the thieves, is that it's fairly easy to avoid detection while selling stolen livestock at auction. Why? The cows often are not branded.

(3)

Why not simply brand the cows? Well, that depends on the rancher. Some ranchers seek support and endorsements from the Certified Humane Project (CHP), and organizations like it, for meat products. CHP grades livestock on a step level from 1 to 5, with 1 being the lowest and 5 being the highest. The higher the meat's rating, the more natural, healthy, and flavorful it is, allowing the farmer to command a premium price. As farmers desire to return to natural and humane ways of farming and cattle raising, while also increasing their earnings potential, fewer farmers are branding their cattle. If farmers treat their animals humanely and get their animals' habitat closer to what normally occurs in nature, the meat will have a higher rating when it finally makes it to the grocery stores.

(4)

One thing CHP has noted is that branding animals is not humane. As such, ranchers have a decision to make—protect the herd with brands or resist branding to achieve higher CHP step ratings. Either choice will likely cost them big bucks.

---

53. What is the main point of this passage?

    A) Cows are expensive.

    B) Cattle rustling is still a big problem for ranchers.

    C) Ranchers should brand their cows.

    D) Meat certifications are big money.

54. In paragraph 2, a rancher is said to have had 100 cows stolen. According to the article, what is the total monetary loss of the cows before processing?

    A) $1,000,000

    B) $10,000

    C) $100,000

    D) $1,000

55. According to the passage, what is a service that Certified Humane Project (CHP) provides?

    A) third-party evaluation of farms and animal habitat

    B) rate livestock and resultant meat products

    C) create benchmarks for organic humane food sources

    D) all of the above

56. The passage implies which is true about branding?

    A) Branding does not affect the animals.

    B) Branding is not a major issue for ranchers.

    C) Ranchers make more money if they don't brand.

    D) Most ranchers brand their cattle.

57. The passage mentions each of the following except _____.

    A) Josey Wales, the outlaw

    B) cattle rustling as "big money" for meth addicts

    C) copper as a source for addicts to fund their habits

    D) services for addicts to overcome addiction

58. Which of the words below most closely matches the meaning of the word *diligently* as used in the first paragraph?

    A) neglectful

    B) persistently

    C) unconcerned

    D) carefully

59. Which of the following is a central dilemma for ranchers?

    A. It's easy to sell stolen cattle undetected because they are not branded, but branding the animals reduces their value.

    B. Ranchers often know the addicts who steal their cattle because they are community and family members, making it difficult to prosecute them.

    C. Branding cattle increases the value of the meat on the market, but it hurts the cows and is not humane.

    D. The Certified Humane Project has been advocating to reduce meat consumption, making it difficult to sell beef.

PASSAGE THREE

(1)

After a person convicted of a crime has served a sentence in a jail or prison, he or she is released back into the community. Prisoner release is a source of relief or frustration depending on individual perceptions, experience, and expectations. Some people believe a person who has committed a crime is lost and can never be **redeemed**. Others believe there are justifiable reasons why any given crime was committed, and thus very few people should go to jail or prison for extended times. Regardless of one's position, when a person has served a sentence, that individual will be released and will return to the community. Moreover, regardless of the opinions of others, the released person often has to deal with fear, confusion, and apprehension.

(2)

So there are many questions that arise. Is it the responsibility of the community to support people who have violated the public trust as they re-enter society? And if so, how do communities support people newly released from jail so they do not become a statistic of recidivism? The answer to these questions forms the basis of re-entry programs throughout the nation.

(3)

Generally speaking, most re-entry programs are composed of various community members and stakeholders. Collaboration between probation, parole, law enforcement, medical and mental health care workers, employment services, housing advocates, clergy, and a host of other services including substance abuse and domestic violence counseling are essential for making the transition smooth and successful. Collaborative partners ensure that resources are set up, or in motion, by the time of release so that participants do not find themselves homeless or re-entering a detrimental living situation immediately upon leaving prison.

(4)

Re-entry programs have shown success in many communities. However, the perceived level of success may be well above or well below expectations, depending on individual **disposition**, the attitude of the participant, and the community in which they now live.

60. Based on the tone of this passage, which is it meant to do?

    A) persuade

    B) share information

    C) admonish

    D) stimulate thought

61. What is an appropriate title for this passage?

    A) Community Frustrated over Prisoner Release

    B) Prisoner Re-entry Programs: What Happens Next

    C) How to Decrease Recidivism Rates

    D) Prisoner Re-entry

62. Based on the passage, it can be inferred that the author believes which of the following?

    A) Criminals should never be let out of prison.

    B) Many crimes are justified, and fewer people should receive long prison terms.

    C) Community involvement is important for re-entry programs to work well.

    D) Re-entry programs work.

63. As used in the last sentence, what is the best definition of the word *disposition*?

    A) bad attitude

    B) frustrations

    C) positivity

    D) natural inclination

64. What is the purpose of the second paragraph?

    A) to illustrate the depth of the issue

    B) to offer a supporting example

    C) to avoid taking a position

    D) to provide more details about the main idea

65. Which is the best synonym for the word *redeemed* as used in paragraph 1?

    A) exchanged

    B) converted

    C) reformed

    D) reclaimed

CLOZE

On this part of the test, fill in each blank with the appropriate word. The words are indicated by blank spaces and dashes within the passage. Each dash represents a letter. The word must be correct given the context of the passage, and it must have the same number of letters as dashes. All words that meet both criteria are considered correct. More than one word may be appropriate for a given space.

All law enforcement officers are sworn in to the office using a standard oath. Each new officer proudly swears that _ _ or she will never betray his _ _ her badge, integrity, character, or the _ _ _ _ _ _ trust, and to uphold all laws _ _ _ the United States Constitution. Every officer _ _ _ _ _ this oath seriously. Most officers will never _ _ _ _ _ _ the day that badge was handed _ _ them and they raised their right _ _ _ _.

The oath is not the only _ _ _ _ _ _ _ an officer makes every day he or she _ _ _ _ on the badge. At each agency there _ _ _ daily reminders of core values, traditions, _ _ _ _ _ _ _ _ rules, the police officers' prayer, and _ _ on. The tenets of each are fairly the same and give an officer _ sense of pride about the job. _ _ _ _ _ _ _ _ such promise is the police officer _ _ _ _ of ethics. The officer code of _ _ _ _ _ _ takes the promise a little further, _ _ _ _ from the law and toward a _ _ _ _ humanitarian purpose. In the code of _ _ _ _ _ _, an officer affirms that his or her "fundamental duty" _ _ to serve humankind, to defend the _ _ _ _ and defenseless against oppression or intimidation, _ _ _ the peaceful against violence and disorder.

It is this last sentence that _ _ most striking. In the midst of _ _ _ _ _ _ around the nation, many might assume _ _ _ officers' role is to intimidate and _ _ _ _ _ _ _ rather than to prevent. Is _ _ possible then for chaos, violence, and _ _ _ _ _ _ _ _ _ to coexist with peacefulness in the _ _ _ _ space, such that any attempt to address violence will not necessarily and negatively _ _ _ _ _ _ the peaceful?

And, if so, how _ _ it possible for an officer to _ _ _ _ _ _ to the oath and the code? _ _ _ _ _ _ _ _, maybe there are two sides to _ _ _ proverbial coin, and both sides of _ _ _ truth are true, even if they may seem to conflict. Meanwhile, _ _ _ can only hope for guidance. We hope also that as we attempt to navigate issues of violence, peace, civil disobedience, and _ _ _ _ _ _ disorder amid the anger, frustration, and mistrust for one another, officers will continue to remember the overwhelming pride and honor felt the day that badge was handed to them, they raised their _ _ _ _ _ hand, and _ _ _ _ _ always to do the right thing.

ANSWER KEY

WRITING

CLARITY

1. **B) is correct.** Sentence A contains a sentence fragment ("Too fast").

2. **B) is correct.** Sentence A contains a misplaced modifier: "on the way to work." It appears as though Steven's car, not Steven, is "on the way to work."

3. **A) is correct.** Sentence B is a run-on sentence requiring punctuation after "party."

4. **B) is correct.** Sentence A contains a vague reference. Officer Daryn says he does not like to drive fast but references an unspecified "you" in the sentence. Sentence B clearly states that it is Officer Daryn who gets sick at high speeds.

5. **B) is correct.** Sentence A contains a sentence fragment. "Unless they become a party to an action" is a dependent clause and must be connected to the preceding sentence with punctuation.

6. **A) is correct.** Sentence B contains a vague reference: "he." It is unclear whether the judge or the defendant was remanded into custody.

7. **B) is correct.** Sentence A is a run-on sentence. A semicolon is required after "staff," or a period should be inserted and a new sentence begun, as in sentence B.

8. **B) is correct.** Sentence A contains a vague reference. Jack calls the Sheriff's Office, which is a business comprised of more than one person but is itself a singular unit; therefore, the use of the pronoun "they" is improper. Sentence B is clearer.

9. **B) is correct.** Sentence A contains a sentence fragment. The phrase "That barks all hours of the day and night" is dependent on the sentence "Greg's neighbor has a dog."

10. **A) is correct.** Sentence B contains a misplaced modifier, the phrase "by Officer Martinez." It appears that Officer Martinez stole the car. Sentence A is written more clearly to show that Officer Martinez made the report.

11. **B) is correct.** Sentence A is a run-on sentence requiring punctuation after "concept."

12. **B) is correct.** Sentence A contains a misplaced modifier. The phrase "eagerly awaiting time off" is a dangling modifier modifying "Ebony's vacation" rather than "Ebony,"

making it appear that the vacation, not the person, was waiting for time off.

13. **B) is correct.** Sentence A is a run-on sentence. Punctuation is required after "safety."

14. **A) is correct.** Sentence B contains a misplaced modifier: "in bags." It is unclear

whether the lunches or the deputies were in bags.

15. **B) is correct.** Sentence A contains a vague reference. It is unclear to whom "they" refers. This sentence illustrates an improper use of the pronoun "they."

VOCABULARY

16. **A) is correct.** *Frantic* means *frenzied*. Choice B, *calm*, is the opposite of *frantic*; it is unlikely a father would be calm if he realized his child was missing. Answers C and D—*frustrated* and *upset*—are both incorrect because it is possible to be frustrated or upset without being frantic.

17. **C) is correct.** *Exacerbated* means *aggravated*, to make something worse. Answer choice A, *hurt*, is not relevant here; it is not possible to "hurt" a problem. Answer B, *reduced*, means the opposite of *exacerbated*. Choice D, *excited*, lacks the negative connotation of *exacerbated*.

18. **D) is correct.** *Verbose* means *wordy*. *Concise* is the opposite of *wordy*. Choices B and C, *clear* and *confusing*, are not the best choices because a text can be clear or confusing while being verbose at the same time.

19. **D) is correct.** To *foster* means to *promote*. Choice B, *create*, is incorrect because it implies the relationships do not yet exist. Choices A and C, *alleviate* and *discourage*, imply the opposite of *promote*.

20. **A) is correct.** To *quantify* is to *measure* or count the value of something. Quantifying something might make it more *understandable*, but answer choice A, *measure*, is the best answer here.

21. **B) is correct.** *Dubious* means *questionable*. *Dishonest*, answer choice A, is not the same as *dubious*; something can be questionable while still being the truth. Answer choice C, *obvious*, is unrelated in meaning. Answer choice D, *definite*, implies certainty, the opposite of *dubious*.

22. **A) is correct.** *Furtively* means *stealthily*. *Fraudulently*, choice B, is unrelated. Answers C and D, *brazenly* and *openly*, are antonyms of *furtively*.

23. **B) is correct.** *Abdicated* is an antonym of *maintained*. Answer choice D, *relinquished*, is a synonym. Choice A, *left*, lacks the implication of a responsible departure; when relinquishing a position, the office holder gives it up to another. Likewise, answer choice C, *abandoned*, is close in meaning but overly extreme; someone can *relinquish* a position or role without leaving irresponsibly.

24. **D) is correct.** *Deviate* is the opposite of *remain*. The other answer choices—*diverge*, *depart*, and *sway*—are synonyms of *diverge*.

25. **C) is correct.** *Guile* is the opposite of *honesty*. Answer A, *duplicity*, is a synonym. *Assistance*, choice B, is unrelated in meaning and does not make sense in context. Answer D, *savvy*, means clever; someone can be savvy but still be honest.

26. **A) is correct.** *Incite* means to "urge" or "encourage." *Insight* is "the ability to see an underlying truth."

27. **A) is correct.** To *know* means to "have knowledge" of something. *No* is used to show dissent or denial.

28. **B) is correct.** *Steal* means to "take another's property without permission." *Steel* is a type of metal.

29. **B) is correct.** *Affable* means *friendly*. *Friendly* is a more accurate meaning than *warm*, choice A. *Angry*, choice C, would imply

unfriendly, the opposite. *Wonderful*, while positive, is not the same as *friendly*.

30. **B) is correct** *Alienated* means *estranged*. It is likely that her family was also *angered* and *frustrated*, but choices A and C are incorrect because one can be angry and frustrated with a person while still maintaining a relationship with that person. Answer D, *united*, is an antonym of *alienated*.

SPELLING

31. **A) is correct.** Choice A, *adversarial*, is spelled right.

32. **D) is correct.** Choice D, *germane*, is spelled right.

33. **B) is correct.** Choice B, *palpable*, is spelled right.

34. **C) is correct.** Choice C, *subpoena*, is spelled right.

35. **D) is correct.** Choice D, *suspicious*, is spelled right.

36. **C) is correct.** Choice C, *facilitate*, is spelled right.

37. **A) is correct.** Choice A, *interrogated*, is spelled right.

38. **B) is correct.** Choice B, *independent*, is spelled right.

39. **A) is correct.** Choice A, *heinous*, is spelled right.

40. **D) is correct.** Choice D, *incorrigible*, is spelled right.

41. **B) is correct.** Choice B, *perfunctory*, is spelled right.

42. **A) is correct.** Choice A, *seditious*, is spelled right.

43. **B) is correct.** Choice B, *surveillance*, is spelled right.

44. **A) is correct.** Choice A, *tenacious*, is spelled right.

45. **D) is correct.** Choice D, *vagrancy*, is spelled right.

46. B) is correct. The author's main point is that witnesses can be unreliable. In paragraph 1, the author states that "the information officers receive is often inaccurate either because the individual was mistaken in his or her perception, was biased, or was purposefully deceptive." The other answer choices are *reasons* witnesses can be unreliable.

47. A) is correct. The passage implies that officers must diligently investigate due to witness unreliability. The author states in paragraph 1 that officers "must rely on... statements from witnesses and involved parties...to draw conclusions about what actually occurred" during a crime, making choice B incorrect. Choice C is incorrect because that passage states in paragraph 2 that "[t]he most frequent type of unreliable information is mistaken perception," not individual bias. Finally, in paragraph 5, the author states, "It is the officer's duty to use critical thinking, deduction, and logical reasoning to determine what is or is not reliable and why," so choice D cannot be correct; some witnesses can be determined to be reliable.

48. D) is correct. Dishonesty, mistaken perception, and bias are all mentioned in the passage as problems with witness reliability.

49. B) is correct. In paragraph 3, the author writes, "[w]hile some people have biases they are aware of, sometimes people have biases they are unaware of for a number of reasons." People are generally unaware of the bias they hold. The other answer choices are untrue.

50. C) is correct. Paragraph 2 describes auditory occlusion as "a temporary loss or lessening of hearing; sounds are muted or unheard." While auditory occlusion is a sort of sensory disturbance, choice C is better than choice D because it offers a more precise definition. Choice A is incorrect because auditory occlusion is not a *total* loss of hearing, just a temporary loss or lessening of hearing. It is not associated with vision, making choice B incorrect.

51. C) is correct. *Anomaly* means *abnormality*. In the passage, a *time anomaly* is an abnormality in experiencing time. A *commonality* is a shared trait, implying the opposite of *anomaly* in this context, making choice A incorrect. Choices B and D, *ambivalence* and *uncertainty*, have similar meanings and do not make sense here.

52. B) is correct. *Blatant* means *flagrant*. Answer choice A, *obvious*, is close in meaning but is not the best answer, because it lacks the negative connotation of *flagrant*. Answers C and D, *subtle* and *implied*, are oppositional in meaning to *flagrant*.

53. B) is correct. The overall point of the passage is that ranchers still suffer from cattle rustling. The passage addresses the issues of cost, meat certifications, and branding, but these are not the main ideas of the passage.

54. C) is correct. The rancher lost $100,000. Multiply 100 cows by $1,000 per cow: $100 \times 1000 = \$100,000$.

55. B) is correct. According to the passage, "CHP grades livestock on a step level from 1 to 5, with 1 being the lowest and 5 being the highest. The higher the meat's rating, the more natural, healthy, and flavorful it is, allowing the farmer to command a premium price."

56. C) is correct. The passage says that a higher rating from the CHP results in a higher price for meat; the CHP recommends against branding, making C the best choice. In paragraph 4 it is stated that CHP claims "that branding animals is not humane." It can be inferred from this statement that branding hurts the animals, making choice A incorrect. In paragraph 3, the author writes, "[a]s farmers desire to return to natural and humane ways of farming and cattle raising, while also increasing their earnings potential, fewer farmers are branding their cattle." Clearly, branding *is* a major issue for ranchers, and it is unlikely that most ranchers brand their cattle in this climate, making B and D incorrect.

57. D) is correct. Paragraph 1 mentions the points made in choices A, B, and C. The passage never discusses services to help addicts overcome addiction.

58. B) is correct. *Diligently* means *persistently*. Choices A and C, *neglectful* and *unconcerned*, do not make sense; ranchers and law enforcement are clearly attentive and concerned about this issue. Choice D, *carefully*, has a slightly different meaning.

59. A) is correct. In paragraph 2, the passage states that "[t]he problem for ranchers...is that it's fairly easy to avoid detection while selling stolen livestock at auction. Why? The cows often are not branded." However, paragraph 3 discusses how higher ratings from the Certified Humane Project (CHP) mean meat fetches higher prices at market, and in paragraph 4 the author writes, "ranchers have a decision to make—protect the herd with brands or resist branding to achieve higher CHP step ratings." The passage never mentions addicts being members of the community, making choice B incorrect. It explicitly states that branding reduces the value of meat because it results in a lower rating from the CHP, making choice C incorrect. Finally, the CHP is presented as a partner, not an adversary, making choice D incorrect.

60. D) is correct. The main point of the passage is to stimulate thought. It presents a difficult issue: prisoner release. It also addresses two perspectives, noting that "[s]ome people believe a person who has committed a crime is lost and can never be redeemed," while "[o]thers believe there are justifiable reasons why any given crime was committed, and thus very few people should go to jail or prison for extended times." The passage also asks the reader to consider how to support prisoners in the community. Answer B is incorrect because the passage does more than simply provide information—it poses questions in paragraph 2. Answers A and C are incorrect because the passage is objective in its presentation of information and opinion. It never chooses a perspective.

61. B) is correct. Choice B best addresses the ideas of the passage, which discusses the details of re-entry programs. The passage discusses multiple perspectives, making choice A incorrect. Answer C is incorrect because the passage does not mention how to decrease recidivism. Answer D is not the best choice because it is too vague.

62. C) is correct. Answer C is the best choice since the passage discusses the value of collaboration among community stakeholders. Answers A and B are differing opinions explicitly stated in the passage. Answer D is an oversimplification; the author states that "[r]e-entry programs have shown success in many communities" but that "the perceived level of success may be well above or well below expectations."

63. D) is correct. Natural inclination. Answers A, B, and C are incorrect because each can be a natural inclination.

64. A) is correct. Paragraph 2 provokes the reader into thinking more deeply about prisoner re-entry by asking direct questions, illustrating the depth of the issue. The author does not provide an example or supporting details, making choices B and D incorrect. The point of paragraph 2 is not avoidance but provocation, making choice C incorrect.

65. C) is correct. To *redeem* means to "buy back," "recover," "exchange," or "reform." In this context, *redeemed* means "reformed."

CLOZE

All law enforcement officers are sworn in to the office using a standard oath. Each new officer proudly swears that **H E** or she will never betray his **O R** her badge, integrity, character, or the **P U B L I C** trust, and to uphold all laws **A N D** the United States Constitution. Every officer **T A K E S** this oath seriously. Most officers will never **F O R G E T** the day that badge was handed **T O** them and they raised their right **H A N D**.

The oath is not the only **P R O M I S E** an officer makes every day he or she **P U T S** on the badge. At each agency there **A R E** daily reminders of core values, traditions, **C A R D I N A L** rules, the police officers' prayer, and **S O** on. The tenets of each are fairly the same and give an officer **A** sense of pride about the job. **A N O T H E R** such promise is the police officer **C O D E** of ethics. The officer code of **E T H I C S** takes the promise a little further, **A W A Y** from the law and toward a **M O R E** humanitarian purpose. In the code of **E T H I C S**, an officer affirms that his or her "fundamental duty" **I S** to serve humankind, to defend the **W E A K** and defenseless against oppression or intimidation, **A N D** the peaceful against violence and disorder.

It is this last sentence that **I S** most striking. In the midst of **U N R E S T** around the nation, many might assume **T H E** officers' role is to intimidate and **O P P R E S S** rather than to prevent. Is **I T** possible then for chaos, violence, and **D I S O R D E R** to coexist with peacefulness in the **S A M E** space, such that any attempt to address violence will not necessarily and negatively **A F F E C T** the peaceful?

And, if so, how **I S** it possible for an officer to **A D H E R E** to the oath and the code? **H O W E V E R,** maybe there are two sides to **T H E** proverbial coin, and both sides of **T H E** truth are true, even if they may seem to conflict. Meanwhile, **O N E** can only hope for guidance. We hope also that as we attempt to navigate issues of violence, peace, civil disobedience, and **S O C I A L** disorder amid the anger, frustration, and mistrust for one another, officers will continue to remember the overwhelming pride and honor felt the day that badge was handed to them, they raised their **R I G H T** hand, and **S W O R E** always to do the right thing.

APPENDIX
Law Enforcement Spelling and Vocabulary Words

The following is a list of study words and their definitions, as related to law enforcement, for use in spelling and vocabulary.

A

ABDICATE (verb): to relinquish authority or responsibility

ABERRANT (adj.): in an abnormal state

ABIDE (verb): to accept or act in accordance with (a rule, decision, or recommendation)

ABJECT (adj.): low, miserable

ABOLISH (verb): to formally end something, like a law

ABRIDGE (verb): to shorten

ACCOLADE (noun): an award, honor, or acknowledgement

ACCOMPLICE (noun): someone who has helped another person commit a crime

ACCORD (noun): agreement, harmony

ACQUIESCE (verb): to give in or submit

ACUMEN (noun): sound mental judgment

ADVERSARY (noun): opponent

AFFABLE (adj.): friendly; outgoing

AFFECT (verb): to act on; to produce an effect or change in

ALIENATE (verb): to make hostile or indifferent

ALLEGATION (noun): a formal accusation against somebody

ALLEVIATE (verb): to relieve or ease

ALOOF (adj.): distant

AMASS (verb): to collect or gather

AMBIGUOUS (adj.): having more than one meaning or interpretation

AMBIVALENCE (noun): mixed feelings or contradictory attitudes

AMBULATORY (adj.): able to walk; related to walking

ANTAGONIZE (verb): provoke; oppose

APATHY (noun): indifference or lack of emotion

ASSAILANT (noun): one who performs a physical attack

ASSAULT (verb): to physically attack

ASSIGNMENT (noun): a given task, duty, or job

AUGMENT (verb): to increase

B

BELIE (verb): to give an inaccurate impression of; to contradict

BELITTLE (verb): to make someone or something seem unimportant; to denigrate

BELLIGERENCE (noun): aggressive behavior

BENIGN (adj.): not harmful

BIZARRE (adj.): strange; unusual

BLATANT (adj.): obvious

BREVITY (noun): concise speech or writing

C

CAJOLE (verb): to coax or persuade with flattery

CALLOUS (adj.): emotionally hardened

CANDID (adj.): honest

CAPITULATE (verb): to surrender, usually under agreed conditions

CENSURE (noun): condemnation or disapproval, usually formal

CLEMENCY (noun): mercy

COALESCE (verb): to combine into a whole

COERCE (verb): to force by using pressure, intimidation, or threats

COLLUSION (noun): secret agreement or cooperation

COMMISSION (noun): the act of committing; carrying out an action

COMPLACENT (adj.): self-satisfied

COMPLIANT (adj.): obeying, yielding

CONFIDE (verb): to entrust information privately

CONFOUND (verb): to confuse

CONSPIRACY (noun): a secret plot or plan

CONTAMINANT (noun): an impurity

CONTEMPT (noun): disrespect, especially in a court of law

CONTROVERSIAL (adj.): given to debate or argument

CONVERGE (verb): to come together

COPIOUS (adj.): plentiful; abundant

CORROBORATE (verb): to support

CORRUPT (verb): (adj.) to be dishonest or immoral in action

COUNTERFEIT (noun): not genuine

CREDENCE (noun): acceptance as true

CRYPTIC (adj.): secret; mysterious

CURSORY (adj.): hasty

D

DEBILITATE (verb): make weak

DELINQUENCY (noun): actions outside of the law, especially of minors; an overdue debt

DELUSION (noun): irrational belief not rooted in reality

DEPLETE (verb): to use up

DERELICT (adj.): abandoned or neglected, especially property

DETAIN (verb): deprive of freedom

DEVIATE (verb): to depart from the norm

DISCREPANCY (noun): a disagreement between facts

DISDAIN (noun): scorn; contempt

DISINGENUOUS (adj.): dishonest

DOCILE (adj.): manageable; submissive

DUBIOUS (adj.): suspect

E

EDICT (noun): command; proclamation

EFFECT (noun): (of a law) having legal validity

ENCUMBER (verb): to burden

ENTAIL (verb): to involve

EQUILIBRIUM (noun): balance

EQUIVOCATE (verb): to deceive by using ambiguous language

EVANESCENT (adj.): disappearing quickly

EXACERBATE (verb): to make worse

EXCLUSIONARY (adj.): characterized by excluding something

EXCULPATE (verb): to clear from guilt

EXONERATE (verb): pronounce not guilty of criminal charges

EXPEDITE (verb): to hasten or accelerate

EXPENDABLE (adj.): unnecessary; disposable

F

FACILITATE (verb): to make possible; to make easier

FLOURISH (verb): to thrive

FORFEITURE (noun): loss, usually for legal reasons

FOSTER (verb): help develop, help grow

FRANTIC (adj.): emotionally out of control

FRAUD (noun): an act of criminal deceit

FRAUDULENT (adj.): involving criminal deceit

FURTIVE (adj.): cautious; secretive

FUTILE (adj.): unsuccessful

G

GARNER (verb): to gather

GERMANE (adj.): relevant

GLEAN (verb): to collect; to obtain

GRIEVANCE (noun): a cause for complaint

GUARANTEE (noun): promise, especially of repair or replacement for a product

GUILE (noun): cunning

H

HARASSMENT (noun): aggressive intimidation

HEINOUS (adj.): very wicked; offensive; hateful

HINDER (verb): to delay or obstruct

HONE (verb): sharpen

HYPOCRITICAL (adj.): professing feelings or virtues one does not have

I

IMMUNITY (noun): being invulnerable to something

IMPRESSION (noun): a feeling or understanding resulting from an experience

IMPRISON (verb): to confine

INCITE (verb): to stir up

INCONSPICUOUS (adj.): not noticeable

INCORRIGIBLE (adj.): not able to be corrected

INCRIMINATING (adj.): charging or suggestive of guilt or blame

INDICTMENT (noun): a formal statement by an attorney and jury charging an individual with an offense

INITIATIVE (noun): the first of a series of actions

INNOCUOUS (adj.): harmless

INTEGRITY (noun): moral value

IRREFUTABLE (adj.): unable to be denied

J

JEOPARDIZE (verb): to threaten with loss or failure

JUDICIAL (noun): of or relating to a court

JUDICIARY (noun): judges; judicial authority

JUDICIOUS (adj.): having good judgment

JURISDICTION (noun): authority, especially to make legal judgments

JUVENILE (adj.): of or relating to minors or young people

L

LEGITIMATE (adj.): lawful

LENIENCY (noun): mercifulness; acquiescing to someone's wishes

LICENSE (noun): freedom to act; a document granting the ability to perform an action or occupation

LISTLESS (adj.): lack of energy

LUCID (adj.): clear

M

MAINTAIN (verb): to enable to continue

MAYHEM (noun): deliberate injury of someone; a state of violent chaos

MISCREANT (noun): one who breaks the law

MITIGATE (verb): to alleviate

MORBID (adj.): marked by an unhealthy interest in death

MUNDANE (adj.): ordinary, often boring

MYRIAD (noun): a large indefinite number; (adj.): uncountable

N

NARCISSISTIC (adj.): having an inflated idea of one's own importance

NEBULOUS (adj.): undefined in content, form, or limits

NEFARIOUS (adj.): wicked or evil

NEGLIGENT (adj.): characterized by neglect and undue lack of concern

NEGLIGIBLE (adj.): insignificant

NEXUS (noun): a connection

NONCHALANT (adj.): casually unconcerned

NUISANCE (noun): a bother or annoyance

NULLIFY (verb): to void, especially legally

O

OBLIVION (noun): unconsciousness; a state of being unaware

OBSCURE (verb): to make it difficult to see something; (adj.): unclear; esoteric

ONUS (noun): a burden or difficult concern

P

PACIFY (verb): to appease

PALPABLE (adj.): able to be felt

PEJORATIVE (adj.): derogatory; demeaning

PERFUNCTORY (adj.): routine

PERIPHERAL (adj.): on or to the side

PETULANT (adj.): rude

PILFER (verb): to steal

PLACATE (verb): to soothe

PRECEDENT (noun): an event occurring earlier that sets an example

PREVALENT (adj.): widespread

PREVARICATE (verb): to lie; to equivocate

PROCLIVITY (noun): a natural inclination

PROFUSE (adj.): abundant

PROVISION (noun): supplying or providing something; an item that provides sustenance (like food)

PROVOKE (verb): to instigate

PROXIMITY (noun): closeness

Q

QUEASY (adj.): nauseous

QUELL (verb): to calm; pacify; to put an end to; to allay or quiet

QUIRK (noun): an odd trait or behavior

R

RECALCITRANT (adj.): uncooperative

RECANT (verb): to take back; disavow one's opinion or belief

RECIPROCAL (adj.): shared by two parties

RECLUSIVE (adj.): isolated

REDRESS (noun): compensation for wrongdoing

REFUTE (verb): to disprove; to successfully argue against

REPEAL (verb): to revoke; to annul

REPLETE (adj.): full of something

REPROBATE (noun): depraved, unprincipled, wicked person

RESCIND (verb): to cancel

RESOLUTE (adj.): determined

RESPITE (noun): an interval of rest

S

SABOTAGE (verb): to destroy intentionally

SANCTION (verb): give authority or permission to

SAVVY (adj.): shrewd

SCRUTINIZE (verb): to look at closely

SEDITIOUS (adj.): inciting rebellion

SOVEREIGN (noun): high authority, such as a monarch; independent

SPECULATION (noun): reflection on a subject

STATUTE (noun): an act passed by a legislative body

STRINGENT (adj.): demanding strict attention to rules and procedures

SUBDUE (verb): to bring into control

SUBTLE (adj.): delicate; not strong or overbearing

SUCCINCT (adj.): concise

SUPPRESS (verb): to subdue, especially by force

SURVEILLANCE (verb): to secretly watch or supervise

T

TANTAMOUNT (adj.): the same as

TENACIOUS (adj.): persistent; determined

TENUOUS (adj.): weak

THWART (verb): to defeat

TRANQUIL (adj.): calm; content

TRANSIENT (noun): a vagrant; a person without a permanent domicile

U

USURP (verb): to seize

V

VAGRANCY (noun): being without any obvious means of support or livelihood

VERBOSE (adj.): wordy

VILIFY (verb): to denounce; to slander

W

WARRANT (noun): a legal document authorizing police to take an action such as making an arrest

WARY (adj.): cautious; untrusting

WILLFUL (adj.): oppositional; purposeful

Z

ZEAL (noun): excessive enthusiasm

ZEALOT (noun): an excessively enthusiastic person, especially regarding religion

ZEALOUS (adj.): overly enthusiastic

Made in the USA
San Bernardino, CA
22 January 2020